The Declaration of America
and
Other Writings

by
Anthony Jenckes Morse

The Declaration of America and Other Writings

Morse, Anthony Jenckes, 1936-

164 pages

IBSN 13: 978-152279284
IBSN 10: 1522792848

Stellamar Publications
PO Box 315
Johannesburg, MI 49751

Cover background Collage
by Pamela Morse

Piety and conformity to them who like,
Peace, obesity, allegiance to them who like...
I am he who walks the States with a barb'd tongue
    questioning every one I meet.

Who are you that wanted only to be told
    what you knew before?
Who are you that wanted only a book to join you
    in your nonsense?

                    Walt Whitman
                        By Blue Ontario Shore

Table of Contents

Contents

Preface
by the Publisher

It should be said, from the onset, that this is the first preface that I have ever written as a "publisher." Up to now, everything I have written has been as an author, but one who until recently has been dependent on finding a publisher, which of course every would-be author dreams of doing. However, there is a price to be paid for that success, which is the burden of first having to please the publisher in order to have your writing published in the first place. Not that the arrangement is without its benefits, one of them being that the publishers assume the burden of having to successfully promote your book, at least if they want to stay for long in the publishing business.

Recently much of that whole situation has changed, with the advent of what is now widely called "Indie Publishing"– "indie" being short for independent, which very often may be simply as individuals who want to make their thoughts available in print for their friends, or perhaps for a certain niche of the reading public. In fact, I'm beginning to believe that everyone who is capable of giving such an account of their life really owes it to their descendants, and, if they have any talent at all, to those who might benefit from what they write.

In the past, persons with this often very modest goal in mind were often forced to turn to what has been called the "vanity presses", which all too often had the negative connotation of the considerable price one was forced to pay just to see their own words immortalized on paper. Generally speaking this price amounted to hundreds, if not sometimes thousands, of dollars that had to be paid upfront to cover typesetting, proof-reading, etc., etc. In the end, it often turned out to be (as it did for one of my poet friends) a kind of "never again" situation for the would-be author.

The home computer and automated book-printing machines have changed all that, or at least it did for me. After having had some half-dozen books published the old way, I decided to take the "indie" route and since than have published three more books on my own, through the firm "CreateSpace" (an affiliate of Amazon Corporation) all of them advertised and available through the Amazon.com website, and if one wishes, even made available as Kindle e-books involving no paper whatsoever. The total cost of all this is literally nothing – unless you end up asking for someone to design a cover for you or help with editing or the like. All you will have to pay is a very modest fee for any actual copies of the book being sent to you. And if you are content with just reading the Kindle version of your book sent for your inspection before it is pushed, you'll end up paying absolutely nothing! On the other hand, if some one, seeing an ad for your book (Amazon and CreateSpace even provide for overseas advertising and distribution – one of my first sales was to someone in India!) perhaps you may end up even making a modest profit.

Given this discovery of mine, there should be no mystery as to why I alerted my old friend of over the past thirty-some years, Anthony ("Tony" to most of his friends) to this opportunity to have his many essays, articles, and even a few poems which appeared in a local arts council publication, republished all under one cover. And since my increased experience operating a word-processor, and converting files to PDF format, and navigating the CreateSpace website has become almost second nature for me, I volunteered to become, at least for this initial publication, Tony's "publisher"– this under the moniker (derived from my place of residence and the name of my nearly defunct website) "Stellamar Publications".

However, I am also doing this for him for another reason; that being by way of repayment for his promotion over the years of several of my own books, mostly by assenting to write a revue for one (which more than anything else I have written probably represents my boldest attempt to solve theology's greatest challenge – the problem of evil) and later on, prefaces for two others. One of them first involved his reading through about of a hundred and fifty of my short essays to pick a hundred of them for publication, and the final revue – because it involved slogging through my manuscript first before it was published – is now published as a preface to my most recent book. (All three pieces also appear in Part III of this volume).

But even more, not just as a friend but as a theologian, I owe Tony even more for the inspiration, or really, the challenge that his thinking, and especially his love of the anti-theologian, Friedrich Nietzsche, has presented to me. (I still vividly remember being huddled in a small tent with Tony's copy of Walter Kaufmann's study of Nietzsche when an early September wind and rain storm lasting several days left me stranded alone on a small island while on a solo canoe-sailing trip in the Voyageur National Park in northern Minnesota back around 1999!)

Not that Tony or Nietzsche converted me, or even Tony himself, to atheism, but as you will see, in at least a few of his essays, they should make all of us a bit more skeptical of any fundamentalist fanaticism, cheap grace, or, as we are seeing in the Middle East today, the perversion of religion into attempts at empire-building.

Finally – as I should end this to let our author speak for himself – I must say that I still miss having Tony as a distant neighbor (I still live 20 miles farther out in the sticks than he once did). Although his twenty-seven-year retreat into Michigan's north-woods before he returned to his original habitat has instead stretched for me into thirty-four years of increasing solitude, we still manage to visit each other and keep in fairly close touch. So while our callings in life have been very different, I still see myself and him as in some way intellectually and emotionally akin to each other. And so, I highly recommend his thoughts for your own reading and contemplation. I guarantee, he'll make you think.

Richard W. Kropf
Stella Maris Hermitage
Montmorency County, Michigan
December 10, 2015

Introduction
by the author

The main purpose of this introduction is to provide biographical information that will help with the contents and themes of this collection of my essays and other writings.

I was born on December 30, 1936, in Grosse Pointe Farms, Michigan. I attended Grosse Pointe High School, where I graduated with the class of 1955. This was followed by four years at the University of Michigan where I graduated with a Bachelor's degree in Literature, Science, and Arts in 1959. The time between 1960 and 1982, besides military service in the Army Reserve, was spent in the career of retailing: in New York City for four years, and for sixteen years in Grosse Pointe Farms. During that time I married and had two children, a son and a daughter.

However, as I have often said, "It takes a fire, a divorce, and a bankruptcy to clear out the cobwebs from the corner of one's mind!" Hence, at age forty, I moved to northern Michigan, up to my "Walden" of 160 acres, in the woods ten miles northeast of Gaylord (closest neighbor a mile away) with a third of a mile of the famed Pigeon River running through what Hemingway called "the pine barrens east of Vanderbilt", now, for the most part, densely reforested. There, I built (with some help), a new log cabin from trees off the same property. With a view of the river (500 ft. of running water) the interior of the cabin was decorated with old traditional furniture, oil paintings, silver, export porcelain, and leather bound books—many books. Remembrance of things past. Have you ever tried to sell valuable (to you) things? It was the talk of the town; "Where do they get their money?" There was a deck attached to the cabin thirty feet above the river on which for the next 27 years I would do most of my reading, contemplating, and writing.

My main source of employment—I still had to work— was caretaking, "Major-Domo", the Joy estate-Lockwood Lake Ranch (Packard Motor Co.) near Lewiston, MI. My partner, Marie Brabb and I stayed there in the winter—we guarded; they traveled. In the summer I would "work with, not for" my friend Brad Aarons, from Grosse Pointe, who had married Patty, the wife of the deceased Harry Joy, doing all those many things you would do on a 2,400 acre ranch. The two children of Patty and Harry had inherited the ranch. It was all financially handled by Wm. McMillan, of Grosse Pointe and Packard Motor Co. We were all caretakers!

Back at the cabin in the summer, Marie dictated that we must join as community members a service organization. I began by singing a few songs at a Rotary meeting, but it wasn't me. Finally we were invited (you must always be invited) to join the board of the Gaylord Area Council for the Arts serving three counties, Otsego, Montmorency, and Cheboygan. The board members were the cream of the town: lawyers, doctors, high school superintendents, teachers, business owners, etc. The most prominent, for me, was James Stagliano, the great French horn player for the Detroit and Boston Symphony Orchestras (see especially the first footnote to "The Music of an Unsung Hero" in Part II).

Marie, always a "go to the top" organizer, teamed up with the board member who was the music director at the cathedral parish of the Diocese of Gaylord. The new church had a seating capacity close to 800 and was one of the main centers for events as was Hidden Valley-Otsego Ski Club, especially in the summer: among sponsored events were appearances by Detroit Symphony Orchestra, the Traverse City Symphony Orchestra, the Royal Shakespeare Group of

NYC, the Detroit Opera Co., the Detroit Institute of Art, local theater groups, and many more artists and organizations.

I became involved with the literary arm of this council from 1982 when it began until 2002 when it ended. My term as editor of the magazine called "*Art Source*" (not my choice) began in 1985. At first it was published four times a year, then two times a year, and finally once a year, but then much larger than to begin with. This book is the result of some twenty years of writing editorial essays (and a few poems) while selecting entries for each issue. Marie did a beautiful job of designing with color and layout, the most artistic looking magazine of its type. A copy of one issue of the *Art Source* was even pinned to the message board of the McCune Art Center, of Petoskey, Michigan, with a note which read: "This is how an art council magazine should look!"

There are sprinklings of what amounts to my autobiography throughout these collected writings. They are organized into separate categories beginning with "The Declaration of America" which is the longest and my greatest effort. It was published over five years. The final or sixth essay in the series was never published until now. This "Addendum" probably would have ended my editorship but it is the most personal, honest statement on my beliefs. I still stand by it.

The second section or part of this collection consists various other essays and articles arranged in chronological order of publication. As one can see from the list of titles in the Table of Contents, this second section ranges over many and varied topics.

The third section consists of individual book reviews or in one case, a 1992 review of current literature that eventually led to my use of the same title in the fifth of the "Declaration" series, but ends with two book prefaces or forewords which I wrote at the request of my friend Richard (or "Rick") Kropf, who also talked me into letting him publish this collection of my writings. The last "Foreword" — which really began as a review of his manuscript before its publication — is to Kropf's now recently published *Einstein and the Image of God: A Response to Contemporary Atheism*. In particular, I believe, this foreword goes a long way to explaining as well as updating my take on the subject broached in that "Addendum" to Part I.

The final section or Part IV of this collection consists of my poems or more often, free verses, that were inserted among other poems submitted to *Arts Source*.

Yes, I see while rereading all of this that maybe there are too many exclamation marks, too much alliteration and theme repetition (you can make your own list), but I was looking for a certain kind of reader, reading and writing being most important to me. Being editor, I had much freedom even with a board and assistant editors and a wide public. But few complaints!

Sadly, Marie died in 2007. Unlike Thoreau, who had a mother with cookies a mile away, I did not think I would like living in the woods alone. So having two children and five grandchildren living in Grosse Pointe, I returned to my home town.

A few friends (who would never leave and certainly would not have done what I did) joyfully exclaimed: "You're back!" I married the lovely, artistic, Pamela Sattley Morris (did not have to change the monograms) and live in a beautiful colonial house that is originally one half of a 1888 "cottage" then overlooking Lake St. Clair. It was built by Wm. McMillan and was called "Drybrook". We use this historical title still (check out Hawkins Ferry's definitive book on Detroit Architecture). My father was first married to

Doris McMillan, a relative (remember the Joy estate McMillan) who started "The Sign of the Mermaid", the name derived from the Mermaid Tavern near the Globe Threatre where Shakespeare and the boys would meet "under the sign of the Mermaid", in the original McMillan home (Jefferson Ave. near Woodward Ave) and was the purveyor of fine leather bound books (that ended up in my parents library, then up north — remember?) To paraphrase William Faukner's statement "The Civil War is now" – history is now!

An early friend of mine, born in Germany but residing in Grosse Pointe, was one of the most educated (five languages) persons of my generation. He said: "In one's life-time, you must build a house, plant a tree, and write a book." Unlike building the house, planting the tree was easy. Writing a book? Well ... Here it is!

Anthony Jenckes Morse,
December 5, 2015

Part I

The Declaration of America

"The mind of Emerson is the mind of America."
(Harold Bloom)

THE DECLARATION OF AMERICA
I: Work in Progress: American Alternatives

"Oh, brave new world" (Wm. Shakespeare, *The Tempest*)

Visions of a new world, however diverse, existed long before the discovery of America and will exist, in great diversity, in the minds of many long after the close of the 20th century. After its discovery (1492) there would be some fifth generation Americans at the first Continental Congress in Philadelphia (1774) to begin the long struggle for a united, independent nation. John Adams, who would become our second elected president after George Washington, before Thomas Jefferson, describes this first Congress as" a diversity of religions, educations, manners, interest, such as it would seem almost impossible to unite one plan of conduct."

Out of this chaos (not unlike today) bravely emerged the seminal document of our country's purpose: Thomas Jefferson's *Declaration of Independence* (1776). This would be followed by *The Constitution of the United States* (1787), arguments for its adoption, *The Federalist Papers* (1788), and Amendments to the Constitution I-X, *The Bill of Rights* (1791). Not until Abraham Lincoln's *Gettysburg Address* (1863) would there be any further political writings of such importance or influence in shaping the American mind.

Jefferson was a student of the 18th century's European Enlightenment: nature and science as a secular religion. And though in writing his *Declaration* he was really more influenced by the Scottish moral-social philosophies of David Hume and Francis Hutcheson that would oppose the more harsh, secular, materialistic edge of John Locke, we are probably politically freer in interpreting the *Decla-*

ration of Independence as a Lockean, Enlightenment defense of the individual.[1]

Even so, Clinton Rossiter will conclude his introduction to *The Federalist Papers: Hamilton - Madison - Jay* (1961): "And the message of the Federalist reads: no happiness without liberty, no liberty without self-government, no self-government without   constitutionalism, no constitutionalism without morality — and none of these great goods without stability and order."

Morality set upon a foundation of stability and order is a prerequisite for all values to follow. But what is the morality of this foundation? What does it do? What does it say? Jefferson gives us in his *Declaration* only a moral guide by which we are fated free to pursue our own moral system. Jefferson knew that a body of persons (government) could only legislate for or against our lower political nature. He also knew that only the single, unfettered person outside government might be brave enough to legislate, only through language, for or against a higher morality. We can through the *Declaration of Independence* and *The Constitution of the United States* discover for ourselves, if we choose to, what moral documents we might hold to be the Declarations of America.

To help us in this matter of discovery, we must understand the importance of the written word to these political founders. They were students of the word. They considered language and its modes of dissemination (writing and printing) to be the supreme inventions of mankind. In that age of dawning technology, they thought the principle mark of human ingenuity was still the ancient skill of verbal communication.

And what else do we have of these political founders than their words? Though we entered the New World with nature as a guide, we have evolved and continue into the 21st century to evolve in this New World with language as the new guide. With our purpose so defined, what writings, what moral documents, what Declarations of America can we claim to be so primal, so seminal, so sacred to Americans that being such could be added to that illustrious list of founding political documents and their creators be called founders, fathers, saints?

There are three writers of such moral weight whose writings fall between the last of the founding political documents and Lincoln's famous address: Ralph Waldo Emerson, Henry David Thoreau, and Walt Whitman. As obvious to some as these names might be, it is only most recently (1960's, 70's) that they have been newly enlisted in advanced studies of language so that they have now been called founders of American culture and philosophy (Harvard's Stanley Cavell), Fathers of American literature (Yale's Harold Bloom) and American saints (City University of New York's Alfred Kazin). This new recognition will carry them well over into the 21st century — new revelations from old writers of America's historical and moral purpose instilled in the continuous study and practice of language that Jefferson and the other founding political fathers promised to protect.

To facilitate and to underline the reasons for including Emerson, Thoreau, and Whitman on the list of American founders, I'm going to borrow, from Jefferson's Preamble to his *Declaration*, the headings "Life" (Emerson); "Liberty" (Thoreau); "Happiness" (Whitman). With these three glorious words to guide us, I will show why these three writers more than fulfill, in ways Jefferson himself could never have predicted, his greatest wish: the freedom to follow one's higher moral nature only in ways that would enhance for all the spirit and beauty of this "New World." Jefferson did know though that with his *Declaration of Independence* he was laying the foundation, with the freeing of our political nature, for an American alternative, which with its freeing of our higher moral nature would reveal in its collection of documents a higher language of morality — thus our Declaration of America.

EMERSON: LIFE AS THE MIRACLE OF MUTABILITY

No one was more timely suited, better prepared, or professionally determined to fulfill Thomas Jefferson's vision for America than Ralph Waldo Emerson. Born in 1803, the year Jefferson presided over the Louisiana Land Purchase (roughly one-third of our present size) from the French for $15,000,000, Emerson died in 1882, twenty years after Lincoln spoke at Gettysburg, twenty years before the birth of my father (my way of keeping our recorded history a matter of a short time, making past events contemporaneous, history being now!)

Jeffersonian themes of the Enlightenment would be repeated in Emerson's first essay *Nature,* 1836. But to accept Emerson as Jefferson's natural heir solely on Enlightenment principles, to rely on those anti-establishment, secular, and propertied ideals espoused by the founding fathers is to miss the spiritual side of their intentions only hinted in their political declarations, a spiritual side that Emerson and those who followed would bring to perfection.

In Nature, Self-Reliance, and *The Divinity School Address* we have the beginning ideals presented in these first Declarations of America. Emerson's great themes of nature as guide, the sacredness of the individual, the infinity of the human mind, the principle of non-conformity, Man as method — a selecting principle are given expression in these first declarations.

Every student should be acquainted with these ideals. Yet it might surprise many that outside high school and college survey courses with their respective anthologies, Emerson had not been read seriously after the early part of the 20th century, had not been given recognition as a philosopher, a philosopher of language, let alone the founder of American culture, American philosophy or American literature.

Beginning in the late 1960's and early 70's there would be a revival in Emersonian studies and an interest in the Emersonian Tradition: Thoreau, Whitman, Dickinson, Frost, Stevens, Ashbery to give only the poetic line. Emerson is now entrenched as an original thinker and founder and is considered the most influential writer of 19th century America, guaranteeing his propulsion into the 21st century.[2]

The three writers / philosophers / critics who I have found to be the most helpful to me in this discovery of the Emersonian Tradition are: Richard Poirier of Rutgers University, Harold Bloom of Yale University, and Stanley Cavell of Harvard University. I will begin with Richard Poirier, mainly because of the three he has written the single most accessible work on literature, literature and criticism in America, and the Emersonian renewal and its effects for the future.[3]

To begin with, Poirier has given me the most succinct statement concerning Emerson's relationship to those above disciplines that have been reworked and combined: "Both in his effort and in his significance Emerson is essentially a philosopher of language and literature. He is at once totally obsessed with language and totally convinced that literature is the place where the obsession is apt to occur most consequentially."

This produces a politically conservative position (that Harold Bloom, more than anyone else, will take over from Emerson) and brings us to one of Poirier's main arguments of his book: the strength of the passive, non-assertive and reconstructive position of the revived Emersonian Tradition compared to that of the aggressive, ideological, nihilistic and deconstructive stance now being taken in Europe by the followers of Nietzsche, Foucault, and Derrida. "While Emerson uses, as do they, a vocabulary of revolution, none of them (Emersonians) can or wants to imagine a revolution except one that might change human consciousness through the revolutions or tropings of words. . . . The revolution worth pursuing is the continuous act of turning and overturning the page."

This is the real difference, this relation between literary and political action, that separates American and European approaches to literary studies as we enter the 3rd millennium. And my main point is that through the likes of a Poirier, Bloom, and Cavell, with the support of an Emersonian Tradition, America will not be the weaker of the two with its less willful, benign stance.

In summary and to conclude this first part I must stress Poirier's Emersonian and democratic defense of Literature, his reasons why Literature should make the strongest possible claim on our attention: its wide social and historical base, its shared principles and deep resources, its great gregariousness in the common conduct of daily life. Works of art, music, film may sometimes be more enjoyable and certainly show equal genius. But in explicating meaning, either toward nullification or toward fulfillment, nothing is superior to Literature. "To Literature is left the distinction that it invites the reader to a dialectical relationship to words with an intensity allowable nowhere else, which

Technology, especially in the form of video, cannot offer in any sustained way, and which many kinds of writing are quite anxious to abridge. Despite its own affiliations with Technology, and perhaps because it feels guilty about them, Literature tells us not that we are in "the prison house of language" but that we are on parole."

In delusion we are tooled up, "on line," basking in binary bliss; certain and secure. In reality, so ambiguous, so mutable, we are out on our words only. And only Literature approaches our ever elusive guaranties of enlightenment, totalities of truth, promises of salvation. Only Literature approximates our lasting needs.

---

[1] For an interesting and informative reinterpretation of Jefferson as a moral and social philosopher see Gary Wills, *Inventing America, Jefferson's Declaration of Independence,* (1978). See also his Pulitzer Prize winning *Lincoln at Gettysburg.*

[2] A personal aside may help to give this discussion some perspective. The last two courses I took as a student of philosophy and literature were on "Extistentialism," a primarily European phenomenon, given then (1960) by visiting (from Princeton to Michigan) professor, translator, and philosopher, Walter Kaufmann. Among many things, Kaufmann was most responsible for reintroducing and re-interpreting Frederick Nietzche (also influenced by Emerson!) to post World II America as a more benign thinker than the image earlier fostered by Nazi Germany. Nietzche's influence as a philosopher of language later promoted by Heidegger, Foucault and Derrida was then, under Kaufmann just being scratched. And Emerson's name was never mentioned.

The English department under which I studied was still heavily influenced by T. S. Eliot and his southern agrarian fellow critics and poets. This was the reigning literary influence (that repressed or ignored the Emersonian tradition) reaching back some 50 years and labeled "New Criticism."

[3] *The Revival of Literature, Emersonian Reflections* by Richard Poirier, Faber & Faber, London, England, 1990.

(Art Source , January, 1995)

10

Work in Progress_

The Declaration of America

II: American Aesthetes, Regal Readers

"It is remarkable that involuntarily we always read as superior beings..." Ralph Waldo Emerson, *Essays*, "History", 1841

Finding Emerson, Thoreau, and Whitman founders firmly anchored in those noble documents of our country's beginnings is to make the play and study of their, and now our, supreme language, with its great themes and sublime utterances, the final goal of our endeavors, and given so little time to life (Emerson), liberty (Thoreau), and happiness (Whitman), the only pursuit. Thus I conclude Part I[1] and introduce Part II.

LIFE: *"I am a fierce Emersonian."* Emerson in Bloom

Described as "the most ardent of Emersonians"[2], Yale University's Harold Bloom is America's most distinguished literary critic, a person of immense learning, scholarship, originality, and productivity. I am continuously surprised at the reccurring references to, and the overall influence of Emerson that permeates his work. The adulation is heightened when we discover through Bloom the company Emerson keeps in Western literature: Dr. Samuel Johnson, Wm. Hazlett, Walter Pater, John Ruskin, Tho. Carlye, Oscar Wilde, and those Emerson influenced: Wm. James, Charles Peirce, John Dewey, Friedrich Nietzsche, Sigmund Freud (through Nietzsche) and all American .writers after him.

"The mind of Emerson is the mind of America." And Bloom adds that Emerson is the "American difference" in its approach to poetry, literature, criticism and pragmatic post-philosophy, his influence and theories underlying all subsequent American writing. "Of Emerson I am moved to say what Borges said of Oscar Wilde: he was always right."

Emerson, the father of the American philosophy of Pragmatism, is the philosopher of power—American style—whether literary, spiritual, political, or economic because he espoused the idea of ever crossing, the theory of the transitional: never to rest with ends but move always with means: "Life only avails, not the having lived. Power ceases in the instant of repose; it resides in the moment of transition ..." ("Self-Reliance," *Essays*). It may be for better or for worse to have the philosopher of power the primary influence in the formation of the American mind and Bloom both celebrates and laments this fact: "Admittedly, I am happier when the consequence is Whitman's "Crossing Brooklyn Ferry" than when the Emersonian product is the first Henry Ford, but Emerson is canny enough to prophesy both disciples."

It is high irony, when speaking of power, that the two most influential thinkers of the 19th century on the 20th century, Nietzsche and Marx should be so represented in the two thinkers who founded American culture, Emerson and Thoreau. I continually come across references to the influence that Emerson had on Nietzsche. Stanley Cavell, for one, not only talks about Emerson's "decisive philosophical influence" on Nietzsche but also states that "Emerson's presence in Nietzsche's thought is so strong at certain moments that one has to say that Nietzsche is using Emerson's words." This influence, "Nietzsche's undying debt to Emerson," for Cavell, is also directly related to Heidegger, considered the greatest philosopher/thinker of the 20th century. Thoreau was not in any way a direct influence on Karl Marx, but his writings reflect the same concerns with social injustices and economic distortions with which Marx dealt and Thoreau presents prescriptions that echo Marx (with more humor). The double irony is this: American thinkers among Europeans are

12

hardly ever honored or given recognition. And social, economic, and religious criticisms that are socially and politically repressed in this country are nestled securely in survey textbooks in American high school and college curricula.

We must all of us keep coming back to Emerson because he is so basically and originally what being an American is all about. What drew me to Harold Bloom is that while he is so thoroughly immersed in Western literature and pursues literary criticism through so many highly complex systems of thought— Gnoticism, Orphicism, Kabbalism, and Freudianism—he returns always to Emerson who while an American so amazingly and profoundly filters, foreshadows, and fulfills in a language that reflects his powerful, pragmatic American style, these thought systems thrusting them to new heights, providing new possibilities.

Since we have had over the last two decades an Emersonian revival, this leads Bloom to conclude that Emerson, not Marx, Nietzsche, or Heidegger (or their French descendants, Derrida et al), will, with his spirit of the democratic individual, guide our criticism in the future. And though we are prone to an economic and social individuality, physical and rugged, it is in our imaginative lives that Emerson's vision most applies. The goal of Bloom's criticism is to goad us into living that life.

To illustrate how Bloom incorporates the spirit of Emerson into his interpretive work, I will highlight his theory of the Reader's Sublime, the reader's ability to know, appreciate, and enjoy nobility, greatness, and beauty, or as I will call it, the American Aesthete as the Regal Reader, of the American aesthetic experience. This should have an even wider appeal than his theory of the Anxiety of Poetic Influence, as famous and important as it is, for to be guided by Bloom, once you have mastered his assimilated terminology through his critical maze, is an education onto itself. But first and foremost, the art of reading is a must prerequisite for any form of study, or for that matter for any form of understandable living.

Emerson read for what he called the "lustres," Walter Benjamin called the "aura," Freud called the "omnipotence of thought," Bloom calls the "Sublime," and I call the American aesthetic experience, Emerson's declaration of America being his challenge for one to lead a life of nobility and beauty. In an important chapter, "Emerson: The American Religion,"[3] Bloom quotes from Emerson's essay, "Self-Reliance," "my own favorite Emersonian sentence": "In every work of genius we recognize our own rejected thoughts; they come back to us with a certain alienated majesty." These majestic thoughts are the reader's own sublimity, own knowing, own rhetorical response as it was once Emerson's. After him, our literary and religious mind has followed no other path. He gives us our interior voice, our American spirit of language. As close readers, we share in his aesthetic experience for to know it not leaves us with his warning: "Those men who cannot answer by a superior wisdom these facts or questions of time, serve them. Facts encumber them, tyrannize over them, and make them men of routine, men of senses, in whom a literal obedience to facts has extinguished every spark of that light by which man is truly man..." (*Essays*, "History").

For Bloom, the above reader does not read with love and disinterest, but tendentiously, politically. "To read in the service of any ideology is not to read at all. You must choose. Either there are aesthetic values or there are only the over determinations of race, class, and gender." In an era of political correctness, multicultural movements, and feminist interpretation this makes Bloom, in literary matters, a conservative. Yet, he insists in his most recent book, *The Western Canon - Books and School of the Ages*, 1994, that he is not concerned with the debate between right-wing defenders of the canon "who wish to preserve it for its supposed (and nonexistent) moral values," Wm. Bennet's *The Book of Virtues* and *The Moral Compass* are good examples, and that "School of Resentment" (academic-journalistic network-Bloom will not misuse the word "liberal") "who wish to overthrow the canon in order to advance their supposed (and non-existent) programs for social change." The works of Alice Walker or Marilyn French would serve this "school."

This I surmise is tantamount to mixing politics with religion which for Bloom is the beginning of a devaluing of aesthetic standards. The aesthetic is autonomous and cannot be reduced to ideology or to metaphysics. Bloom argues for the autonomy of imaginative literature and for a reader - solitary, sovereign, soulful. He thinks that this soul in its inward quest to be free and solitary, reads only to confront greatness, to join greatness which is the basis of the aesthetic experience he calls the sublime, a transcending of limits.

In *The Western Canon* chapter," Woolf s *Orlando:* Feminism as the Love of Reading," Bloom repeats Emerson's refusal of historical conditioning and displaces Virginia Woolf' s supposed founding of Feminist literary criticism with her aesthetically founded love for and defense of reading and provides us with her "most authentic prophesy": "No one since Hazlitt and Emerson has possessed that passion so memorably and usefully as she did. No other twentieth-century person-of-letters shows so clearly that our culture is doomed to remain a literary one in the absence of any ideology that has not been discredited. Religion, science, philosophy, politics, social movements: Are these live birds in our hands or dead, stuffed birds on the shelf? When our conceptual modes abandon us, we return to literature..." Since *The Western Canon* is also an elegy, this is, for Bloom, a note of optimism. "Doomed" here means ultimate failure for whatever ideology held, leaving us with an aesthetic fate, painful and difficult, but offering pleasure and satisfaction (without solace) nevertheless. *The Western Canon,* being a short course in Bloom's critical theories and applications, is a brilliant exercise in aesthetic judgment only. It is also a heroic defense of the Reader's Sublime in spite of the fact that today any "canon" is viewed as elitist, hierarchical — an anathema to the academy.

In *The Western Canon,* Emerson is Bloom's implicit guide where he is not his explicit guide, one reason being that both are Americans. Dr. Samuel Johnson is the "Canonical Critic," but Emerson being a purveyor of wisdom like his precursor, Montaigne, is the canonical guide. After all, Bloom has never said of Johnson what he has said of Emerson: "I revere him!"

Canon-formation is not arbitrary but born of the human need for judgment, rational, supportable and an aesthetic hierarchy of values. It favors reading that restores meaning rather than destroys meaning. Bloom sees this particularly in Emerson's American process of re-centering as opposed to Nietzsche's (or Heidegger's) European process of de-centering that has led to deconstructionism. Both Emerson and Nietzsche have looked into the abyss of nihilism but only Emerson, the American, has given us new reconstructive reasons to read. For the reader this can be a religion of language of meaning which is always open as opposed to a religion of words of dogma which is always closed.

Bloom keeps repeating how Emerson and the Emersonian tradition is the great counter-force, the American antibiotic to the disease of deconstructionism imported from Paris. But Bloom, himself, is the main alternative, and as deconstructionism comes to its own creative and critical dead end, he will be recognized for the successful battle he has begun and is finishing.

Since we are fated free and thus responsible first to make a method of our own mind, which is only and all that is available to us, the task of the text requiring close and deep reading will then reap multiple results: pleasures and rewards that accrue in the reader's aesthetic experience. This is an open invitation to participative reading and I, for one, who have invested heavily, can attest to its allurements and frustrations, to its promises and fulfillments. But Bloom does not hide from us the darker side of this noble occupation-that the art of reading as the authentic aesthetic experience may be waning, is waning in Emerson's America.

Bloom describes this problem as a "falling-away from text-centeredness" or even "text-obsessiveness" that was once so much the center of American Jewish culture and American culture generally though maybe not with the same intensity. It is an ancient Jewish belief that holiness can be achieved through the study of the Torah (the Hebrew Bible). Bloom points out that this is not a Biblical idea as usually believed but Platonic, Plato's idea being that our salvation lies in a love for learning, a love for texts. "If that love (for some text, any text) vanishes, and probably it will, then the other love (for a more difficult, religious text) will never come."[3] (*Agon*, 1982) This echoes the concerned mentors adage that any kind of reading is better than no reading though "text" dictates some discernment. If this bleak prophesy prevails, what hope is there for the rest of America who do not have as severe a reverence for "text-centeredness," for the love of learning as the American Jew?

If our past belongs to Emerson, our only hope is that so must our future. And if Harold Bloom can so convincingly convey the idea of the Reader's Sublime based on Emerson's "lustres," surely we can rise to the task of the text and come to know our own aesthetic supremacy. We have no choice. Vacuity and violence await us; culture and civility elude us. We will not have full freedom until we have aesthetic freedom. Materialist and ideologue have this still to learn from

Emerson and Bloom. Only in and through a vision for the human being, for being human, like that provided by Ralph Waldo Emerson and refined and celebrated by Harold Bloom, can we possibly reach the transcendent grandeur we were destined to achieve. We were born to be American Aesthetes, Regal Readers.

---

[1] Part I: "The Declaration of America: American Alternatives," *Art Source,* Winter 1995-96.

[2] Richard Poirier, Ibid.

[3] *Agon: Toward A Theory Of Revisionism,* H. Bloom, 1982.

(*Art Source*, Winter 1997)

THE DECLARATION OF AMERICA

III: Liberty and Thoreau: Ordinary Language and the Sacredness of the Secular

A friend of mine, when we are discussing great poetry and high matters, has on more than one occasion told me how for many years he was under the illusion that Portia's famous speech, "The Quality of Mercy," in *The Merchant of Venice*, was adopted from the King James Version of the Bible. To the orthodox, this is a natural assumption of Shakespeare's homage to the Bible, of the secular to the sacred, a proper appropriation of Holy Writ by ordinary language.

Though I haven't made the same assumption as my friend, I have always felt that Henry David Thoreau's *Walden* is a religious work and its author a most spiritual being. Unlike the orthodox, I have not attributed this work ("genuine Scripture, the nation's first epic," Stanley Cavell) to any outside source, but continue to be amazed by the originality of its creator.

The literary critic and scholar Harold Bloom reminds us that the concepts sacred and secular are only sociopolitical designations. All attempts to call any strong work of literature more sacred than another are merely political and social formulations and say more about us than the work itself. This is a truth that underlies the cultural conflict that is now ensuing in America, that literary works are only to be distinguished aesthetically, that is, how well they serve the great, the noble, the beautiful.

More specifically, Bloom insists that no text fulfills another text, that any such appropriation is an insult to the originality, independence, and integrity of the work in question and if such a work of literature obtains to national stature, it is finally an insult to the people for whom it was originally intended. This can only happen when there is no dissolving of the secular into the sacred or the sacred into the secular. One example, for Bloom, of such an appropriation (and insult) would be *The New Testament's* subsumption of *The Old Testament* (the titles alone a beginning of the problem).

With Thoreau's *Walden*, the problem according to the Harvard philosopher Stanley Cavell, is not improper appropriation and subsumption but total neglect, secular or sacred interpretations notwithstanding. Even Harold Bloom neglects Thoreau though he maintains his name in his tight canon of 19th century American writers: "Emerson's one surly follower who was also a genius in his own stance and right whose one consistent teaching was the Emersonian insistence upon continuous intellectual effort." This is the extent of his interest. For Bloom, American originality begins with Emerson, and the most important Emerson-based prose writers are Wm. James, Charles Peirce, John Dewey, and most recently Richard Rorty, "the most interesting philosopher in the world today." As the American "Prince of Pragmatists," Richard Rorty, for Bloom, culminates the long line of Emersonian thinkers. And this compliment is in many places in Rorty's writings repaid by a seconding of some of Bloom's ideas and theories. This mutual admiration society (of two) is one of the leading forces in American intellectual circles today. The importance of Rorty's culmination of Emersonian Pragmatism will be taken up in a concluding essay, but for now, we must ask, where does this leave Henry David Thoreau?

For an answer, we have to turn to Stanley Cavell if we want to find the most innovative approach to Thoreau to date. For Cavell, Thoreau heads the list of "founders of American thinking, American Philosophy" with Emerson, a close second: "Thoreau's

Walden is the major philosophical text of my life - other than *Philosophical Investigations* (Wittgenstein)." *(In The Quest of The Ordinary,* 1988). The Emersonian, Harold Bloom, being so immersed in Biblical study, so dedicated by virtue of his Jewish inheritance to the great originality of the Book of Moses — now related in his acclaimed *The Story of J* — does not recognize the great American and Scriptural epic that *Walden* is. Stanley Cavell does.

Cavell stands in a long line of praiseworthy criticism for Thoreau. And in my readings of Thoreau criticism, I have never (until Cavell) found a more stunning single statement of praise than Stanley Edgar Hyman's: "At his best Thoreau wrote the only really first-rate prose ever written by an American, with the possible exception of Abraham Lincoln; and as a political writer, he was the most ringing and magnificent polemicist America has ever produced." ("Henry Thoreau in Our Times," *The Promised End,* 1963) I read this many years ago and believed it. I believe it still and only marvel now that with the inclusion of Lincoln, how it complements the founding theme of *The Declaration of America.* Yet, in the annals of Thoreau criticism, it maybe his own mentor Emerson who, in his "Thoreau," his great prose elegy, wrote the best single, sustained piece on him (again with the exception of Stanley Cavell).

Like Cavell, I came to Thoreau before Emerson. Being the great writer that he is, Thoreau is more accessible than Emerson and smatterings of his writing that adorn so many cultural artifacts have lured many to become faithful readers of his works. I would like before turning to Cavell, to add to the above collection three of my favorite sentences from *Walden,* three sentences that probably due to their length have never, to my knowledge, been extracted for edification or inspiration, three sentences that for time and space will give us the flavor of the man of whom we so highly speak: "Some of you, we all know, are poor, find it hard to live, are sometimes, as it were, grasping for breath. I have no doubt that some of you who read this book are unable to pay for all the dinners which you have actually eaten or for the coats and shoes which are fast wearing or are already worn out, and have come to this page to spend borrowed or stolen time, robbing your creditors of an hour. It is very evident what mean and sneaking lives many of you live, for my sight has been whetted by experience; always on the limits, trying to get out of debt, a very ancient slough, called by the Latins Aes Alienum, another's brass, for some of their coins were made of brass; still living, and dying, and buried by this other's brass; always promising to pay, promising to pay, tomorrow, and dying today, insolvent; seeking to curry favor, to get custom, by how many modes, only not state-prison offences; crying, flattering, voting, contracting yourselves into a nutshell of civility, or dilating into an atmosphere of thin and vaporous generosity, that you may persuade your neighbor to let you make his shoes, or his hat, or his coat, or his carriage, or import his groceries for him; making yourself sick, that you may lay up something against a sick day, something to be tucked away in an old chest, or in a stocking, or, more safely, in a brick bank; no matter where, no matter how much or how little." (Chapter 1, "Economy")

"Some of you," indeed. We cannot, none of us, say "not I." "Aes Alienum" is a finer etymological sounding of our condition than Marx's Alienation of Labor theory and nowhere in Marx will you find a so poignant and poetic crescendo against false necessity as you will here. This lamentation to our condition begins Thoreau's transformation, for us, of the secular into the sacred, his redemption, for us, of the ordinary, of the every day. *Walden* is not only a guide to this success - *Walden* is success. And Stanley Cavell guides us through this success being its most insightful expositor.

One of the continuing problems concerning the proper placement of Thoreau is our persistent attempt to think of him only as a nature writer. Surely, he is one of these and is properly acclaimed as the father, founder, and inspiration of the environmental movement that grew out of the 1960's. And this is due mainly to the deep philosophical and spiritual base in his writings that we so casually acknowledge. But neither Thoreau nor Emerson were ever treated seriously as philosophers until Harold Bloom (Emerson as founder of American literature has vast philosophical implications[2]) and Stanley Cavell came upon the scene.

Though both Thoreau and Emerson are found in all of Cavell's work, the starting point emphasizing Thoreau is his *The Senses of Walden* (1992): "The most searching study of *Walden* ever written. *The Senses of Walden* is proof that Thoreau and Emerson have not only established but also inspired a tradition of American thinking." *Thoreau Journal Quarterly.*

Politically, spiritually, and literarily Cavell compares Thoreau's *Walden* to Plato's *Republic,* Hobbes[1] *Leviathan,* Locke's *Second Treatise of Government,* Rousseau's *Social Contract, Discourse on the Origin of Inequality* and *Emile,* to Kant, Hume, Marx, Nietszche, Kierkegaard, and Wittgenstein, to the *Old* and *New Testament,* the *Bhagavad Gita,* and the *Vishnu Purana,* to Christ and Buddha, to Sophocles's *Oedipus at Colonus,* and Milton's *Paradise Lost* and Coleridge's *Ode to Dejection,* to Homer, Chaucer, Dante, and Wordsworth.

This impressive and formidable list points up Cavell's seriousness in including Thoreau in the profession of philosophy, his interest in linking philosophy to literature and will induce many to return to *Walden;* it should not intimidate anyone who will first find superb descriptions of nature, continuous homespun humor, and down to earth philosophy in which we all, all the time, participate. This is the basis of

Cavell's Ordinary Language Philosophy of which he is today the most famous proponent and he enlists Thoreau and Emerson as its prime practitioners, ahead of Heidegger, Wittgenstein, and Austin.

The problem of Thoreau's and Emerson's acceptance into the tradition of philosophy is addressed more fully in Cavell's *In the Quest of the Ordinary* (1988): "There has been no serious move, as far as I know within the ensuing discipline of American philosophy, to take up Emerson and Thoreau philosophically. The moral to draw here may of course be that Emerson and Thoreau are to be comprehended as philosophical amateurs, toward whom, it would be implied, there is no professional obligation. But suppose the better moral is that Emerson and Thoreau are as much threats, or say embarrassments, to what we have learned to call philosophy as they are to what we call religion, as though philosophy had and has, an interest on its own behalf in looking upon them as amateurs, an interest, I think I may say, in repressing them. This would imply that they propose, and embody, a mode of thinking, a mode of conceptual accuracy, as thorough as anything imagined within established philosophy, but invisible to that phi- losophy because based on an idea of rigor foreign to its establishment." ("The Philosopher in American Life")

The name Cavell gives to this "foreign rigor" is reading and this should give us all inspiration, we American aes- thetes, we regal readers. This reading process, as Cavell explains, is not to inherit philosophy as a set of problems to be solved (as Anglo-American analysts do) but as a set of texts to be read (as Europe does — the Continental Tradition). Since Cavell covers many other subjects relating Thoreau and Emerson to the current scene, underwriting Wittgenstein, Heidegger, and others in Modern Philosophy, I concentrate, here, as I have elsewhere, on the simple but important topic of reading, hoping to make what I point out as relevant and interesting as possible to everyone.

The importance of reading is most profoundly analyzed by Cavell when he approaches this sentence of Thoreau's: "Could a greater miracle take place than for us to look through each other's eyes for an instant?" Cavell calls this miracle of taking each other's eyes in reading and writing, the "fantastic," exalting Thoreau's vision of our ordinary lives being "incredible and astonishing"; that our ordinary lives are fantastic and our language a most mysterious medium. Of all the writers who have presented this idea of the holy union between reader and writer, none, according to Cavell, have gone beyond Thoreau in persistently and systematically noting that the reader of the book, not the characters in the book, is "fantastic," is all that he or she would want to be and mean.[3]

Of the secular and sacred, there is unity; of the reader and writer, there is unity. This is the beauty and greatness of *Walden*, that, through this inestimable source, we will find ourselves, know ourselves, follow ourselves in searching out what is necessary and not necessary, thus providing the maximum of "American liberty," in our lives. No less than the other great works of philosophy, reading *Walden* will give us all (as writing it did for Thoreau), an occasion for thinking and thanking.

[1] *Art Source.* "The Declaration of America, Part I: Jefferson and The Emersonian Tradition: American Alternatives," 1994-95.

[2] For an expanded text of Cavell's "Philosophy of the Fantastic," see "Fantastic News," *Art Source,* 1991.

(*Art Source,* 1998)

Work in Progress

THE DECLARATION OF AMERICA
IV: Happiness: Walt Whitman's Unyielding Yelp

"Democracy has its seer in Walt Whitman." John Dewey

Out of my Rhode Island past, out of this blue vein of blood streaming, then famously, now gloriously (our blood, in propensity and property, democratically reducing us to the commonality of salt water) to the sky blue sea; out of this mixture of myth, memory, and metaphor, the fanatical Baptist and first governor of Rhode Island, Roger Williams, out of his own theological intolerance, first instituted religious freedom in America, ingeniously warding (wording) off the potential destructiveness of his own thinking.[11]

This legislation for religious freedom along with John Adam's fear and hatred of organized religion (the Church of England) and Thomas Jefferson's "wall of separation" set the stage for a freedom and religiosity in America unknown to the rest of the world.

From all this, Ralph Waldo Emerson, evolved, with his pragmatic experiment, followed by Henry David Thoreau and Walt Whitman, a line of thought, most American in its evasion of abstraction and theory, most American in its empirical and materialistic application, and most American in its secular idealism and spirituality.

The third founder of this American spirit of power, provocation, and personality Walt Whitman, is the least discussed, in the matter of pragmatism's development. Because he comes upon the scene of founding a little later (but still within the vision of Lincoln—literally and figuratively) and because he is in poetic disguise, Whitman is also excluded from the discussion of the founding of American philosophy in general. But even more than Emerson and Thoreau, Whitman through his literary achievement originally introduces and poetically captures for the public imagination many of the themes of American pragmatism, philosophically and spiritually.

Though he doesn't take, in total, this particular stand on Whitman, I must first go back to Harold Bloom[2] for the most recent and strongest defense of Whitman, if not as a founder of an American philosophy, then at least as a founder (with Emerson and Thoreau) of American literature.

With the possible exception of the prose of Henry David Thoreau and the poetry of Emily Dickinson, *Leaves of Grass*, by Walt Whitman is the greatest work of literature written in America by anyone, anytime, anywhere. For Harold Bloom, all world literature begins and ends with Shakespeare. For him, all American literature begins with Emerson and ends with Whitman.

From his chapter "Walt Whitman as Center of the American Canon," (*The Western Canon*, 1996) Bloom begins: "To find their (the strongest poems of *Leaves of Grass*) aesthetic equivalent in the West one must go back to Goethe, Blake, Wordsworth, Holderlin, Shelly, and Keats. Nothing in the second half of the nineteenth century or in our now almost completed century matches Whitman's work in direct power and sublimity except perhaps for Dickinson... Shakespeare centers the Western canon because he changes cognition. Whitman centers the American canon because he changes the American self and the American religion by changing the representation of our unofficial selves and our persuasive if concealed post-Christian religion."

This "American religion" of Bloom's I take to be the flowering of pragmatism which culminates for him currently in Richard Rorty, the poet philosopher who resides symbolically at Thomas Jefferson's University of Virginia. Rorty will offer us the final appreciation of Whitman.[2]

In the annals of Whitman criticism, it is Emerson who first states a most accurate judgment: "I find it *(Leaves of Grass)* the most extraordinary piece of wit and wisdom that America has yet contributed." These words still stand.

In more recent years it has been an Englishman not an American who has provided us with the greatest appreciation of Whitman. In his now classic *Studies in Classic American Literature,* (1934) D. H. Lawrence states that "Song of the Open Road" is the key poem of Whitman's monumental *Leaves of Grass.* Outside of its famous and optimistic opening ("Afoot and lighthearted I take to the open road"). Whitman does not hide the darker side of life, embraces death (Lawrence's most praising point), recognizes evil (something Emerson is unjustly criticized for ignoring) and mocks the puffing, primping, (and pimping) social and religious habits that sometimes surround us: "Behold through you as bad as the rest, Through the laughter, dancing, dining, supping, of people, Inside of dresses and ornaments, inside those washed and trimm'd faces, Behold a secret silent, loathing and despair… Smartly attired, countenances smiling, form upright, death under the breastbone, hell under the skull-bone... Allons! the road is before us! It is safe — I have tried it — my own feet have tried it well — be not detained! Comerado, I give you my hand! I give you my love more precious than money, I give you myself before preaching or law; Will you give me yourself? Will you come travel with me? Shall we stick by each other as long as we live?"

In homage to Whitman, Lawrence produced his own strong prose poem: "Whitman, the great poet, has meant so much to me. Whitman, the one man breaking a way ahead.

Whitman, the one pioneer. No English pioneer, no French, no European pioneer-poets . . . Ahead of Whitman, nothing. Ahead of all poets pioneering into the wilderness of unopened life, Whitman. . . ." And Bloom comments: "Lawrence helped foster the American critical tradition of always rediscovering the actual Whitman, the great artist of delicacy, nuance, subtle evasiveness, hermetic difficulty, and above all else canonical originality. Whitman founded what is uniquely American in our imaginative literature."

Though Bloom thoroughly examines Whitman's diversity and influence in that first chapter, he devotes a second chapter on what he sees as Whitman's "most vital influence," one upon South American literature, surely one of the strongest contributions made in the 20th century. In "Borges, Neruda, and Pessoa: Hispanic-Portuguese Whitman," Bloom confirms Whitman's position as the center of the American canon: "He is the poet of our climate, never to be replaced, unlikely ever to be matched. Only a few poets in the language have surpassed 'When Lilacs Last in the Dooryard Bloomed': Shakespeare, Milton, perhaps one or two others."

After Harold Bloom's most inspiring support, we can only go to Richard Rorty for the most recent innovative appreciation of Walt Whitman. In his latest book, *Achieving Our Country:* "Leftist Thought in Twentieth-Century America," Harvard University Press, (1998), Rorty takes a sabbatical from his spirited ruminations on American pragmatism to attempt a rejuvenation of an old style of politics: participative, active, reformist, a style reminiscent of Teddy Roosevelt and the Progressive Era that set the tone for America's high democratic achievement in this century. In turning away from this old style, the new cultural left with its emphasis on theory and ideology is inactive, academic, and spectatorial. It is divisive with its multicultural, ethnic, feminist, sexist departmentalization.

It is the politics of justice, real issues, of which Walt Whitman and John Dewey are for Richard Rorty the foremost spokesmen in this country. Rorty agrees with Kenneth Rexroth, the grandfather scholar/poet of the Beat Generation, that Whitman invented the idea of "the realization of the American Dream as an apocalypse, an eschatological event which would give the life of man its ultimate significance.... It is the last and greatest of the American potential."[3] Only Rorty would add that Dewey is the last. For both Whitman arid Dewey, democracy is a kind of religion: "Whitman and Dewey were among the prophets of the civic religion (real politics). The most striking feature of their redescription of our country (not spectatorial and retrospective but political agents for a better future - achieving our country) is its thorough going secularism (anticlericalism rather than atheism). Pragmatism is to be compatible with religious belief-but only with a privatized religious belief, not with the sort of religious belief that produces churches, especially churches which take political positions." Whitman did not ask for divine favor or wrath: "And I call to mankind, Be not curious about God, For I who am curious about each am not curious about God."

"The priest departs, the divine literatus comes," said Whitman. For Emerson, Thoreau, Whitman, and Dewey, works of the secular imagination replace scripture as the principle source of inspiration and hope for each new generation. And writers like Bloom and Rorty have for the most recent generation refined, in a most intimate and exacting way, this vital message.

I came to this study by chance five years or so ago, discovering first with Thoreau, mainly with Emerson, and finally with Whitman that there had been a major revival, a renewed interest and a developing philosophy around these three "transcendental," "classic" writers who were a major part of the "American Renaissance." As important as these terms were, and still may be, these early writers, founders, in the street and in the schools were, for all practical purposes, dead — buried in the "Grand Tradition." But now, at last, they have been resuscitated, resurrected, new blood poured into old veins. Emerson, Thoreau, and Whitman roam again departments of literature, criticism, philosophy, cultural studies, and whatever other interdisciplinary studies that may be in the making. They are dressed in Harold Bloom's aesthetism; in Stanley Cavell's ordinary language philosophy; in Richard Rorty's pragmatism. Of more importance, they are alive again in the streets of America, even if for now only in Harold Bloom's "persuasive if concealed" forms — as life, liberty, and happiness.

And they give us warning. Emerson: "He who has a thousand friends has not a friend to spare. And he who has one enemy will meet him everywhere."

And they present us reality. Thoreau: "The greater part of what my neighbors call good I believe in my soul to be bad, and if I repent of anything, it is very likely to be my good behavior... There is no odor so bad as that which arises from goodness tainted ... I never dreamed of any enormity greater than I have committed. I never knew, and never shall know, a worse man than myself."

And they make us witnesses. Our bloodiest contest, the Civil War that defines us still, defined Walt Whitman. He was the nation's "Wound Dresser" and the war's Homer: 'I am the man, I suffered, I was there." So when friends, family, and the faithful are usurped and assimilated (as they always are) to any cause, we need not just look at what might be an obvious threat, but also be ever vigilant to that appeal that promotes our good. To aid us in this vigilance, we will always have recourse to these persons presented above — these nonbelievers who are true-believers in their declarations of America — and in an achieved America, we need not rely on this little ditty to set us free:

> Once far away and long ago
> Stories told what's ever so:
> Humpty Dumpty and the Raven
> "Never again" and "nevermore"
> Neither heaven nor a haven
> But rings truly in the heart's core.

---

[1] For an insightful rendering of this matter, see Garry Wills *Under God,* 1990.

[2] For the kind of politics Rorty would not support see my review of *God: The Evidence* by Patrick Glynn (1997).

[3] For a good study of this subject see Betsy Erkkila's *Whitman: The Political Poet,* Oxford University Press, 1996.

(*Art Source*, Winter 1998-99)

THE DECLARATION OF AMERICA
V: Tutelage Two Thousand: Reading

"To read well, that is to read true books in a true spirit, is a noble exercise, and one that will task the reader more than any exercise which the customs of the day esteem. It requires a training such as the athletes underwent, the steady intention almost of the whole life to this object. Books must be read as deliberately and reservedly as they were written."

Henry David Thoreau, "Reading", *Walden*, 1854

My father taught me that life requires a proper tutelage: that being, by his definition, one's life long duty to self-education. He would underline this important point with the classical concept, proclaimed first by the ancients, that an educated man is a rich man. I simplified this to the commandment: read for life!

This theme is kept alive in the writing of a current few, one being the editor of *Harper's* magazine, Lewis Lapham. In one of my favorite commentaries on the contemporary scene, his monthly erudite "Note Book," Lapham continuously reminds us of the ease with which people assign to money the power of imagination and intelligence and he maintains that this idea must be challenged. (He reminds us again in his latest book of wit and profundity, *Lapham's Rules of Influence: A Careerist's Guide to Success, Status, and Self-Congratulation*, Random House (1999). Considering his background and current position, Lewis Lapham knows well whereof he speaks.[1]

Out of our American past, variations on the above theme have been famously noted: Emerson's belief that the only "sin" is to resist mental growth; Thoreau's disdain for intellectual laziness; Lincoln's lifelong contempt for the idea that accidents of worldly rank imply a hierarchy of intrinsic worth. In a specific example of this spirit, Thoreau, in his immortal ode to the ordinary, *Walden*, shows that the crystallization of the mind is the result of voluntary simplicity (and in reverse, that the focused mind will dispense with the diversions and distractions of vacuous and inconsequential things). The most famous example of this spirit though is Walt Whitman choosing symbolically for his acquisitiveness a common leaf of grass and calling it "the flag of my disposition" in his monumental *Leaves of Grass*. The leaves of this essay, before you, I submit, are added support to all the above and are, indeed, the flags of my disposition.

When Aristotle compares the educated and the uneducated with the living and the dead, he is laying the foundation for his proclamation that education is the best provision for old age. In stating this, he must have known that self-education is inextricably tied to aging, one redeeming the other. This process creates a sense of attentiveness and immediacy (if not urgency) that is born of our evolving knowledge that we must, to paraphrase the Bard, endure our coming hither, our going hence.

With the above in mind, I view religious, cultural, and educational institutions with the due respect they deserve, but must acknowledge also the limited value each has in supporting life. In accordance with Jefferson's ideal of enlarging the franchise and enhancing life, these institutions are a great guide at best when availability and opportunity prevail and are something less when they do not. Even successful matriculation through any institution misleads if it is applied as a badge and not as the basis for continuing self-education. Self-education is an Archimedean point that gives all the leverage needed to lift our world.

Given the limitations of institutions and the current confusion noted above as to what our true interest should be, I have been pursuing as sources for self-education the following themes[2]: pragmatism as the American philosophy (Emerson); the sacredness of the secular and the aestheticism of the ordinary (Thoreau); the universality of democracy (Whitman); and the value of close, reflective reading which can only explicate and enrich these themes (Rorty and Bloom). I have consolidated these related themes into one concept: that of the pragmatic/aesthetic reader.

The simplest meaning of pragmatism is practical experience pursuing truth, of aestheticism the study and appreciation of beauty. The pragmatic/aesthetic reader, as self-educator, evolves out of the tradition of responsibility, integrity, and independence which has been proven necessary and sufficient in the past and will prove to be the same for the future. The terms pragmatism and aestheticism may sound oppositional and incompatible, but, when observed in operation, they are complimentary and facilitate the full functioning of each other's merit. The aesthetic approach is the most pragmatic; the pragmatic approach is the most aesthetic. Without the one you will not have the other.

The practice of being a pragmatic/aesthetic reader can be interpreted on a wide scale as any reading that serves our needs, that works for us, that gives us pleasure, that supports our beliefs and desires, that shows us finally in Keats's lovely line that "truth is beauty, beauty truth." It can be used to support the most mundane career goal, the most sectarian ideological cause, and the most metaphysical abstract system of unity (or disunity). On a narrower scale, pragmatic/ aesthetic reading can take on the guide lines of specific thinkers, in this case, of two thinkers most respected in their fields who represent this dual concept. The renowned philosopher, Richard Rorty, is most responsible for the revival of pragmatism in this country. And

Harold Bloom is the leading literary critic in America who makes aestheticism the center of his work.

Again, we can take Rorty/Bloom (and their respective work) as guides to an understanding of pragmatic/aesthetic reading. And again, Rorty/Bloom, as with pragmatic/ aesthetic reading, cross over each other in that their respective work is best understood by each other's discipline. In one you have the other. I will first discuss the Rorty/pragmatic half of the coupling and then finish with the Bloom/aesthetic half to further advance our understanding of this reading process.

The three most repeated criticisms directed at pragmatism are: that it perpetuates relativism; that it undermines systems of value; and that it is shallow. The short reply to these criticisms is that no thinking person who calls him/herself a pragmatist would deny that his or her views are true (the rhetoric that we offer others is the absolute we offer ourselves), nor deny that thinking itself creates a hierarchy of values (the ultimate one being honesty, specifically intellectual honesty), nor deny, finally, the intrinsic shallowness of positions that cannot be proven true or universal (no pragmatist has gone further to point this out than Richard Rorty). Relativism, value diminution, and shallowness are red herrings and as criticisms of pragmatism simply do not hold up.

Pragmatism is, in part, a process of criticism and we could paraphrase Shakespeare's Iago by saying that we are nothing if not critical. Of course, I would leave Iago to his nihilism, take the hope-filled high ground and proclaim pragmatism and criticism as synonymous with living and thinking: we are nothing if not critical.

Below, above, or through this pragmatic process one will continue to dream, hope, desire and believe as much and as long as one's conscious (and subconscious) will allow. This is the human condition. The principles of this very American philosophy of pragmatism are imbedded in the founding documents of our country. I have shown, using Jefferson's preamble to his Declaration, that our founding thinkers (taking their lead from the Founding Fathers) began to define the concepts of pragmatism: Emerson—life as method; Thoreau—liberty as righteousness; Whitman—happiness as means and ends.

There is also a continuing tradition in America of further ground-breaking and liberating voices of pragmatism: Charles Sanders Pierce who applied the rigor of science to ideas: William James who emphasized experience, "the stream of consciousness," and the "cash value" of ideas; Oliver Wendall Holmes who proclaimed that the life of law was not logical but experiential; John Dewey who made both science and experience the foundation of our public education system; and finally Richard Rorty, the poet-prince of pragmatism who revitalized this most American of philosophies by emphasizing "aesthetic consciousness," showing that literature and art follow from the principles of pragmatism. Rorty is a very prolific and exciting writer who has turned from being an academic philosopher (University of Virginia) to a popular public philosopher. For Rorty, we are a crowned consciousness of cares and causes, centerless and contingent, coping, conversing. With his high profile, Richard Rorty is a great example of how pragmatism engages art, ideas, and public affairs as he leads American philosophy into the 21st century.[3]

Now to the Bloom/aesthetic half of this dual concept. The traditional criticism directed at aesthetic activity is that it can lead to "decadence" (whatever that means!). The traditional answer to this is Friedrich Schiller's *Letters on the Aesthetic Education of Man* (1800), in which he shows (following Kant) aestheticism to be the most comprehensive attitude available. Everything else — economics, politics, morality — is subsidiary to the aesthetic sense which is, after all, grounded in human freedom.

Even more than Richard Rorty, the "Colossal Critic" Harold Bloom relies on the founding thinkers, particularly Emerson and Whitman, to support his aesthetic theories. And while both Rorty and Bloom are the most recent and prominent thinkers to combine aestheticism with pragmatism, we can find similar combinations in those above mentioned founders Emerson, Thoreau, and Whitman. In fact, in all my previous discussions on these thinkers, I never mentioned the term "transcendentalism" in reference to them and concentrated only on the pragmatic and aesthetic aspects of their writings. The term tended to repress interest and when dropped was one reason for the revival of these thinkers, particularly in academia.[4] I'm going to suggest that what is usually taken to be "transcendental" yearnings in these thinkers' works by past commentators are mostly the workings of the aesthetic imagination. Transcendentalism as traditionally represented is now a repudiated philosophy but William James, John Dewey, etc, and now Richard Rorty and Harold Bloom never depended on this supposed philosophical aspect of Emerson's, Thoreau's, or Whitman's work. What they saw and took into their own views was a much stronger combination of pragmatism and aestheticism. Bloom's reading of Emerson and Whitman is the finest example of this syncretic process. He shows that there are between pragmatism and aestheticism, to paraphrase Shakespeare's Hamlet, more things of heaven and earth than we have dreampt of in any philosophy.

Harold Bloom of Yale University is the foremost practitioner of aesthetic theory in America. He compliments Richard Rorty in that he takes a pragmatic approach to each literary work he discusses before ending in an aesthetic appreciation. As Rorty uses literary/aesthetic references throughout his work, Bloom relies on pragmatic principles as a foundation upon which he builds his aesthetic work, offering us his "Reader's Sublime."

Bloom's most recent work, his magnum opus of a life-time of study and teaching is *Shakespeare: The Invention of the Human*, 1998 (a New York Times Best-Seller). It is a superb and profound example of an aesthetic appreciation, pragmatically applied, the pragmatic/aesthetic reader at work, an education unto itself. In his introduction, Bloom, with self-effacement, gives us an inescapable reason for mastering this reading process: "I am naive enough to read incessantly because I cannot, on my own, get to know enough people profoundly enough."

The pragmatic/aesthetic reader is the final combination of Bloom's Reader's Sublime, Rorty's Crowned Consciousness, and what I earlier (Part II) called the American Aesthete as Regal Reader. Without such idealistic and exalted descriptions (firmly grounded), how else are we to inspire and celebrate reading for the young, how else than to make reading the highest of life's fulfillments? This reader, like King Lear's only noble daughter, Cordelia, ends the 20th century wanting nothing, comes into the 21st century asking nothing. Wanting nothing, asking nothing: the only practical foundation from which to observe truth and beauty. The pragmatic/aesthetic reader as the tutorial guide into the year 2000 and beyond makes readers in a democratic America, in a democratic world, people first among people.

---

[1] See Lewis Lapham, *Money and Class in America* (1992).
[2] See Parts I-IV "The Declaration of America", *Arts Source*.
[3] See Louis Menand, *Pragmatism: A Reader*, Vintage Press (1997).
[4] For the most up-to-date history of the "detranscendalizing" of Emerson, see Michael Lopez, *Emerson and Power, Northern Illinois Press* (1996).

(*Art Source*, Winter 1999-2000)

Addendum

THE DECLARATION OF AMERICA
Credo — Non Credo
In Morse Code

"My, those essays you've written in ' The Declaration of America' are remarkable — intensely literate and probing, showing your reading mind in great depth! They're really impressive evidence of all you've worked on over the years. I enjoyed reading them a lot. . . And I am most grateful for your eloquent elucidation of his (Harold Bloom's) — and through him of Emerson's, Thoreau's and Whitman's — thought. Your passion and his passion — are contagious. *Bravi tutti!*

   "Still the truth is that, although I genuinely admire the 'aesthetic reader' you admonish us to become, and although in savoring great philosophical texts, as I do, I feel the elevation you hope we'll feel in the presence of greatness, I can't espouse this as a sufficient end in itself. Perhaps it's the scientist in me. Transitions are fine and proper and being 'on the way' is a noble mode of being, but combining these with getting some place is even better!

   "I've been struggling so long as a philosopher that I'm grateful to find now that besides appreciating (and loving to teach) my beloved texts (most of them hallowed classics — Plato, Aristotle, Epictetus, St. Thomas, Kant, Hume, and even some moderns like James and Royce and Dewey, Husserl, Whitehead, Sartre and Merleau-Ponty), I've achieved at least some very secure beliefs about what matters to me."

   This is the latest and most substantial review (in the form of a letter from John Compton) that I've received on my essays "The Declaration of America". I have quoted him at length to show his sensitivity concerning the problems and joys in pursuing philosophy as a way of life. This and his praise and the reservations have inspired me to write an addendum — not so much to refute polemically his critique, but to seriously investigate his suggestions (with poetic license) and speak more personally and explicitly for myself, all in the spirit of friendship. It is difficult for an amateur like me, with degree (BA Intellectual History, University of Michigan), to answer a philosopher, teacher and former head of the philosophy department at Vanderbilt University, Nashville ("A world class university with an international faculty", James Howard Kunster). But, as John Compton knows, philosophy has been made up, at times, of less than sterner stuff.

A further paragraph from Compton will show the complexities of wending one's way through the pleasures and tasks of the text and provides a possible meeting ground for the two of us:

> "Of course, I'm still re-writing, but I'm grateful that I've come to see certain things more clearly than before - how there is mysterious creativity all around us, how we exist as thinking, feeling, yet thoroughly bodily beings, how we are totally dependent upon and need sustainable relations with the natural environment, how we are inevitably part of each other as equal members of a world community, how the future possibilities for each of us depends upon those for all the others. While I love the solitary pleasures of the text, I find I need an increase of substantive understanding more."

All of this is very powerful and thus I will treat it as "The Text". To start, I want to know (another letter from John Compton might help) what "secure beliefs" and "substantive understanding" can he not get from the "beloved texts", the "hallowed classics" of his long vocation and longer avocation?

Further than the written text, the visual and audible arts, and all the roving blood and beauty about us, I can only surmise (and he suggests) that the source might be technical and scientific. If so, then I must borrow (for now — can I have it both ways?) from the Book of Job, the greatest anti-theological and anti-metaphysical tract ever, in which God asks: "Where wast thou when I laid the foundations of the earth? Who hath laid the measure thereof? Who hath stretched the line upon it"?

I concur that the "pleasure(s) of the text" (a Roland Barthes title and charmingly the name of a book store, *Le Plaisir du Text*, on the Isle de St Louis, Paris) and the tasks of the text are solitary, but so is most of life, particularly as we mature (grow up, not old!) and these texts really become important. These pleasures and tasks which can have romantic and difficult aspects for the "aesthetic reader" are no less goal-oriented than those pursuits of scientific interest that John Compton may be examining — a study of the mind of our "thoroughly bodily being" — a great and important part of philosophical interest these days.

I accept also the "mysterious creativity" that surrounds us and on occasion, to stave off absolutes, mumble "preserve the mystery". And I do need "sustainable relations" with some, if not all, that lives and dies, though at every turn I find a humanly-related contingency. And I too am attempting to "get some place" having been "on the way" — a Heideggerian phrase that I once marked "O T W" in books bought in the 1990's. Now it is "GH": Going home!

A friend of mine, a Catholic and catholic to his credit, says humorously that I'm the holder of the "Chair of Nihilism", a fictional academic position. It is a chair, he says, that I hold onto with fear and trembling, white knuckled — ashen. But Nietzsche said that nihilism was "a divine way of thinking". And Emerson, ever popular for his affirmations, in his greatest essays, thought life to be supported by nothing. "As men's prayers are a disease of the will, so are their creeds a disease of the intellect" ("Self-Reliance"). However, nihilism is not my position and acquaintances will attest to my optimistic, good (God) natured disposition. For me, aestheticism (love of beauty, from which, all else follows — economics, politics, morality — the theme of Friedrich Schiller's "Letters on the Aesthetic Education of Man" following Kant), underwritten by a restricted form of atheism, is the chair I wish to hold. Aestheticism is a product of the human imagination, evidentially individualistic, materialistic, and verifiable-real (Aristotle). This is opposed to idealism, also a product of the human imagination but evidentially not individualistic, not materialistic, and not verifiable- unreal (Plato). Thus the pragmatic position anchored in that native American ground of founding thinkers like Emerson, Thoreau, Whitman, and our Founding Fathers — the subject of those essays that John Compton read. I don't believe in "nothing" and I don't believe in "everything". I'm an aesthesist!

It is the theism of the Western tradition of a personal God that I object to, not the theism of Aristotle, Epicurus, and the Deist of the 18th and early 19th century: *a dieu faineant* (do-nothing-God) who is not a creator, is not providence, has no awareness of evil, is not in the world, and has no love for man. This is not the God of Abraham (justice), Jesus (love), or Mohammed (only Allah). God's disinterestedness (the unmoved mover!) is infinite. All transcendence is aesthetic imagination!

To Aristotle, "God's thought is thought about thought." Ones' delight in philosophically contemplating the sublime is in God a perpetual state — his only activity — "thinking about thinking (*noesis noeseos*)." God is all metaphysics; we are (thankfully) all speculation. God thinks; man thanks. Who could ask for anything more?

Thinking and thanking have an etymological relationship going back to middle and old English and made stronger by philosophical considerations, one being moral and theological, which is the romantic, poetic concept of the God within. The same Martin Heidegger, a leading 20th century philosopher, who warned of the "waste land within" (below) wrote an important essay, "On Thinking", elaborating on this connection between thinking and thanking. So, starting with the Jewish prophets, the Greek philosophers, and the Roman poets, there is a Western tradition of thinking and thanking that continues with the Medieval mystics, the Renaissance humanists, the Enlightenment empiricists and the Modern literati. This tradition well supplies us with ample guides and beautiful examples for life-affirming conduct.

For all the classic arguments for theism, there are as many equally for the morally noble, intellectually honest, and privately principled position of atheism. And as there is a religious tradition for Judaism, Christianity, and Islam, so is there a long and respected tradition for humanism, secularism, classicalism, and, most abstractly, atheism. Both atheism and theism are abstract terms and the English journalist, Christopher Hitchens ("Love, Poverty, and War" 2005, "God Is Not Great" 2007) is right to insist on the concrete term anti-theist (as opposed to atheist), which introduces the human element into the equation.. At the Apollo Theatre In London (2002) I heard him in an interview on stage say (and reaffirmed in a 20 minute talk with him afterwards) that the real "axis of evil" is Judaism, Christianity, and Islam. What he meant, I think, is that institutionally, dogmatically, humans take to heart (literally and fundamentally, and then politically) the theistic position, oppressing, persecuting and purging (if not spiritually, then physically!) their neighbor in the process, and that this contributes, most significantly, to man's inhumanity to man.

"So many, I had not thought death had undone so many" is T.S. Eliot's line from "The Waste Land", one of the most influential poems of the 20th century, adapted from Dante's "Inferno" ("Divine Comedy") and aptly expresses the continuing slaughter. It is a most powerful poetic line (one of my favorites). Eliot was referring to industrial workers daily walking over the London Bridge (the walking dead) and Dante was referring to eternally suffering sinners in Hell (the wailing dead). For me, the line describes the human condition with a special reservation, emphasizing sacrifice and delusion, for Heidegger's "waste land within" — man's capability to be a wolf unto man. The word god (historically freighted) is no more or less profound than the words all, everything, and nothing (all heavily freighted), and will offend no one when used in an imaginative context, the creation of a fictive force, possessive and personal, that can be poetically liberating and inspirational. But when the word God is attached to a system ("The will to a system is a violation of integrity" — Nietzsche) or to a belief ("I do not believe in belief — Marcel Duchamp) or to a faith ("Faith is an overrated virtue" — Salman Rushdie), then you're approaching trouble! Plato, the idealist, not Aristotle, the realist, banned poets and condemned heretics!

With the mysterious unknown, agnosticism is a proper stance. With an acclaimed revelation though, one must study and seek the best explanation, and short of dogmatism — judge! An agnostic approach, in this case, leads to relativism, little dialogue, and less thinking. Nietzsche's "To judge is the nut of existence" answers the biblical "Judge not, that ye be not judged."

In the final analysis, it is not possible or necessary to reach for metaphysical or theological certainty, for to do so is, in the moral philosopher Bernard Williams' marvelous phrase, to have "one thought too many". We must renounce a final absolute and a final language in science and in religion, since both disciplines are derivatives of philosophy, which teaches us to love the fact that limits are the beginning and the end of wisdom. God is God; God is not and never the twain shall meet. Renounce certainty!

I have become familiar with some of the best wisdom writers because, among other benefits, they acquaint me with not only the past and the present, but also with the future, and in this learning, which is the best, one will live well and long. Such are the intimations of immortality. I can endure the vagaries and vicissitudes of my own disbelief, but not the prophecies and certainties of others. History confirms that their relative revelations, however divined, can be fancifully fulfilled, however deluded, in destitution and death, however justified.

Have I gotten "some place"? Maybe "not yet" (Augustine said evading commitment) but I'm getting closer and though I also seek a more "substantive understanding" I can, at this time, only re-write what I've already written:

> Once far away and long ago
> Stories told us what's ever so:
> "Never again" and "Nevermore",
> Neither heaven nor a haven
> But ring truly in the heart's core.

As an alternative to that "undiscovered country from whose bourn no traveler returns." Hamlet's father enjoins his son to "remember me". This is all one can ever ask of another. Hamlet does and we remember Hamlet (and his last words: "The readiness is all. ...The rest is silence."), so immortalized is he by William Shakespeare. People pass onto pages, if they pass onto any place. That's place enough for me.

46

Thank you, John Compton!

Coda: Related to the indeterminateness of the above discussion, ("no sky hook", says Daniel Dennent, "Darwin's Dangerous Idea", 2002 and "Breaking the Spell", 2005, but we're still hooked to moral choice and responsibility) I recently started a new study: "Henry David Thoreau and The Moral Agency of Knowing" by Alfred I. Tauber (2001, University of California Press, Berkley). It may require me to amend and expand the essay on Thoreau (Part III, D. of A., "Ordinary Language and the Sacredness of the Secular"), which I ended with the "definitive" interpretation of his favorite philosopher, Thoreau, by philosopher Stanley Cavel (Harvard). I hope so. As an heir of the Enlightenment Empiricists, Thoreau, as this study may further show, is still one of the finest examples of life-affirming conduct. Such are the vagaries and vicissitudes of life!

Part II

Other Essays and Articles

"Heaven is under our feet as well as over our heads"
(Henry David Thoreau)

"I am native here and to the manner born"
(William Shakespeare)

I'M A SAUNTERING
1: Singing My Song

I want to reaffirm a sacred and transcendental vision of man in nature that is revealed by the walker in his infinite wisdom and noble activity.... No man is more natural, more essentially constituted, more honest, fine, correct, or finally more noble than a man when he is walking....

To walk is to think, but to think poetically, creatively. The walker by his art becomes *homo poetica*: man the poet practicing his highest calling.... Thinkers have always been walkers. The peripatetic school of philosophy under the leadership of Aristotle thought and taught as they walked. The word peripatetic is Greek, meaning to perform while moving about; the word philosophy is also Greek, meaning the love of wisdom. What is being proven today by science was linguistically established at the beginning of Western culture. Philosophizing should not be under attack. We should question only the mode in which it is done....

Viewing nature from under a bubble stultifies and sterilizes, offering only the glitter and sizzle of the matter. One must saunter and submerge oneself, experiencing fully the earthly elements. We will not then be second-hand Roses, but can say that we were on the scene, into the thick of things—no small achievement in our growing artificial environment.... As long as we choose to be coddled, conformed, and carried by technological devices, we choose a one dimensional mentality that is reductive, repressive, and regimenting. It is also cruel if it becomes a lasting illusion. It is a single vision, seductive in its pleasures, patronizingly comfortable and permissive, and suasively subtle as it divides our human nature. In sauntering through a natural setting, life and death are united to form organic integrity; mind and body are fused to form spiritual integrity. The walker is the physically perfect symbol for a many dimensional process that pulls together the fragmented aspects of our mental and physical world. Walking waxes whole!...

The walker is the supreme conservative; he destroys naught. He is the great liberal; he is freedom incarnate. He is the real radical; he is not party.... The walker is the true conservative in a loose world thought liberal. He is the true liberal in a leaden world thought conservative.... The walker is a revolution unto himself. His meditating, massaging, moving feet are the axis around which turns the mind, round and round with boundless energy, evolving into a deep consciousness, creating a new center for his being, a new vision for his existence—at once beautiful, bountiful, and believable. It is the only successful revolution this world knows, or ever will know. This is a reality and revolution that "realists" claim, of which "romantics" sing, but for us the greatest poverty to know not. It is a revolution of perception and liberation that begins and ends in each man's walk. The whole world will join to call him poet, lover, brother, sage and saint—saunterers all....

There is also a sense of immortality in the process of walking. The hour is not kept; you will live forever in an afternoon's walk. Your soul is the fulcrum/center of the earth. Your individual finiteness is the leverage by which you will see and know the world. In the most real sense, you have not only understood eternity but by the proper proportioning of time through walking, you have lengthened your life. It is a power and glory given us as human beings...

Excerpts from WALKING: THE ART OF SAUNTERING by Anthony J. Morse, Gaylord 1984. (Published in *Art Source*, September/October 1984)

OF PRINT AND TRACKS

Coming upon a set of bear tracks on this year's first snow walk makes concrete some abstract tracking that I've been doing lately. The hind paw measured 5x7 inches which means the bear weighed 350 to 400 pounds. It was noon so I had time to follow the bear's path. The fresh frozen edges of the print indicated that the bear had passed through the evening before. I now had a chance to put into practice some information gleaned from *The Tracker* in which Tom Brown, Jr. shares lessons in survival and tracking that had been passed on to him by an old Apache tracker, Stalking Wolf. I had been tracking Indian lore for some time.

The bear's prints led from tree stump to tree stump but never in a straight line. He (or she but never "it") was looking for grubs that were buried in fallen logs or decaying pine stumps. A bear tracks too—and tracks true.

From another tracking expedition, I remembered William Faukner's "The Bear," a short story considered one of his best works. Circling around, through and over (like a bear) an adventurous hunting tale, Faukner digs into the soul of America, avowing his love for the land while lamenting its diminishing wildness. But my bear was alive and well. He and I were slushing through a new snow in a forest that yearly was regaining its original beauty and mystery.

As time passed, my walk settled into an amused and calm activity—"good medicine," as Stalking Wolf would say. I was being affected by an element of play in the meandering mode of the bear tracks. There was in the gait a relaxed, slow, inquisitive sensibility—making no demand, pressing no dogma, setting no date. From one large white pine stump into which he climbed, he looked casually around in all directions and then climbed down. Tracks can tell all, but as trackers say,

"You have to go to know."

On a more recent tracking excursion, Barry Lopaz (*Harper*, December 1984) revealed in a new way how a specific environment can influence thinking and, therefore, writing. This was important stuff for me, not the stuff of social-determinism or behaviorist thinking, but the real thing —concrete, like grubs for the bear.

Now darkness was closing in. But I had been tracking in this direction long enough. Trails are tender. Care should be taken to preserve the mystery. Our paths will cross again and I will renew my experience with this bear.

There is one danger in all this tracking business that I should mention. Stalking Wolf tells of a tracked bear circling around and coming up behind his tracker, Risks and Rewards, Cover your rear—always. I hear this often and I've even seen it in print. Nevertheless, keep tracking!

(*Arts Source*, Feb/Mar 1985)

A LIBRARY TO MEASURE BY

One can, if one wishes, measure life's transitions in physical terms: houses, automobiles, travels, clothes, restaurants, lovers. T.S. Eliot's pitiful Prufrock "measured out his life with coffee spoons." If measure we must, let me measure out my life with libraries.

The family library: All great libraries begin and end in the home. Seeds are sown; riches are reaped. The high school library (Grosse Pointe, MI): The delight of discovery is nourished with direction. The community library: A modern attempt to express freedom of thought is symbolized by large windows, bright colors and a happy Calder mobile swinging over my reading head. The libraries of Ann Arbor: The excitement and seriousness of reading is raised to a new high. Entering the Law Library was like entering a medieval cathedral. The New York City Library (5th Ave. at Central Park); Rich or poor, the most interesting people in the world, the best of humanity here perform a profound prayer. The Detroit Public Library (Woodward Ave.): A classic architecture of white marble bestowing dignity and elegance upon a noble institution. The Detroit Public Library (Downtown Branch): Under this small roof resides the largest current collection of periodicals in the state. Both of these libraries are designated state resources! Their loyal visitors are as they are in all great libraries: impeccable.

Over the main entrance of the Detroit Downtown Branch is inscribed, "Books are the treasured wealth of the world." This comes from H.D. Thoreau's Walden, in which the chapter on reading begins with, "In accumulating property for ourselves or our posterity, in founding a family or a state, or acquiring fame even, we are mortal; but in dealing with truth we are immortal, and need fear no change nor accident." Books are the bearers of truth; no dust will settle on this revelation.

Today, this tradition is being perpetuated in Gaylord with the erection of a new library building. In dedication, one could do worse than measure our progress by the value that Thoreau places on reading:"To read well, that is, to read true books in a true spirit, is a noble exercise, and one that will task the reader more than any exercise which customs of the day esteem."

Today, a century since *Walden*, knowledge has expanded, scientific knowledge mainly; its contents sifted and refined into new interpretations and revisions; its sources more varied and sophisticated records, tapes, computers and films. Technology will provide new methods for dispersing knowledge and libraries should avail themselves to these services. But the basic source will prevail: "A written word is the choicest of relics. It is something at once more intimate with us and more universal than any other work of art. It is the work of art nearest to life itself." *(Walden)*

This written word, these books, all sources belong to everyone. Hail to the Citizens of Otsego County. You have in your new library your daily pleasure and your eternal measure.

(Arts Source, April—May, 1985)

BEE-ING THERE

"Where the bee sucks, there suck I;
In a cowslip's bell I lie;"

Wm. Shakespeare

The busying bee, the banner of my disposition, goes from flower to flower, sweet to sweet, and fulfills the job that we in part began, the perfection of our gardens. He is inspector and guarantor of our sometimes frustrating but noble effort. He is the official appraiser of our art.

That gardening is an art, a sacred art even, is attested to in modern environmental tracks as well as sung in ancient poetry and mythology. We might not need to be reminded of this, but the bee reminds us, nevertheless, and in his meandering lies a message.

For in the plying of this art we come to understand the meaning of simplicity, that somehow it is related to happiness. We also gain a reverence for all life. In this single act of cultivating the earth we draw together all the material elements that surround our life — sun, water, air and minerals. It is a silent, motionless and most mysterious act, this growing process, and from it we derive all the nourishment we should ever need, physical and spiritual.

It is an activity that has appealed to the most sovereign of minds, pursued by those in the highest office. Thomas Jefferson wrote to his friend Charles Peale in 1811: "No occupation is so delightful to me as the culture of the earth, and no culture comparable to that of the garden. Such a variety of subjects, one always coming to perfection, the failure of one thing repaired by the success of another, and instead of one harvest a continued one through the year. Under a total want of demand except for our family table, I am still devoted to the garden."

Gardening is at once an act of poetry and prayer; it is also simply an act of doing. Thoreau who had other worlds to attend confessed at Walden: "I did not read books the first summer; I hoed beans." The bee made sure of it.

(*Arts Source*, June/July 1985)

Footnotes... IMAGES, INFORMATION, AND ILLITERACY

"We are such stuff as dreams are made of..." W. Shakespeare

"Where is the knowledge that is lost in information?" T. S. Eliot

We are what we imagine; the world is that which we conceive. This august axiom of ancient wisdom and modern physics, of religion and psychology, reigns above all determinate and indeterminable influences that condition humanity. Furthermore, we are fated free to choose those very images that we can control through our will to truth or have controlled for us by the art of self-deception. These are given variables to given verities. One image we are choosing to change, under the illusion that we are pursuing the truth, is the one that guides us in how we communicate images themselves: the written word. Responding to this change, the August 1985 issue of *Harper's* magazine, conducted a symposium on the "Decline of Literacy". It is a growing problem that affects 30 to 66 million Americans depending on which set of requirements for literacy is being used. One must go to the magazine to find all the reasons why this is happening. But, at the center of this decline lies the "Information Revolution". In turning to the dark side of the soul, the human spirit is experiencing a desert of dryness and despair. And the light side?—George Stiener, educator, concludes, from the same issue, in his "Future of Reading":

> *What about reading in the old, private, silent sense? This*
> *may become as specialized a skill and avocation as it was in*
> *the scriptoria and libraries of monasteries during the so called*

> *Dark Ages. We now know these were in fact key ages, radiant*
> *in their patience, radiant in their sense of what had to be*
> *copied and preserved. Private libraries may once again become*
> *as notable and rare as they were when Erasmus and*
> *Montaigne were famous for theirs. The habit of furnishing a*
> *room with shelves and filling them with books;... the attempt*
> *to collect the complete editions of an author (itself a very*
> *special concept) with the hope of owning everything by a*
> *writer whom one loves; the ability - above all the wish - to*
> *attend to a demanding text, to master the grammar, the arts*
> *of memory, the tactics of repose and concentration that great*
> *books demand; these may once more become the practices of*
> *an elite, of a mandarinate of silence.*

Maybe, with medieval methods, we can again preserve the mystery and miracle of contemplative reading which is nothing less than an act of redemption: build an impenetrable bulwark, dig a deep and wide moat, draw up the bridge, batten down the door—all this against the unholy onslaught. Thus we make a hermitage of our home, a mansion of our mind, an island of our images. Ours is a monastery moderne, as mighty and majestic as the medieval Mont Saint Michel on its secluded islet; and we its mod-mad monks, contemplatives complete, who have become a beacon light to legions of illiterates, waiting for this plague, a puffball pretending substance, to smoke out.

(*Arts Source*, October/November 1985)

Footnotes...

I KNEW HIM, HORATIO

Genius would become a common virtue if we but relaxed, took time and observed the notes of nature. Shakespeare teaches us this when he expands upon autumn to symbolize the last cycle of life "when yellow leaves, or none, or few, do hang..." Those "few" do remain, even through the worst of wintry blasts, and Shakespeare's lovely sonnet too.

When Hamlet to Horatio laments the fate of "poor Yorick", it is more than dramatic propriety that induces Shakespeare to be specific, to note names. He is also drawing out and involving the persons behind the names. And ultimately, "alas", it is you and me that Shakespeare is addressing. He knows our names — keynotes — have a sound like no other sound.

At an October convention held at Boyne Mt., Rollo May, the renowned psychologist[i], spoke on the importance of human vulnerability in the role of all counseling. Our magnificant Michigan fall colors were not lost on Dr. May: "Leaves are a species of death... Beauty comes out of death... We heal each other by virtue of our own wounds." It was nice to hear, see and speak to Dr. May in his autumn appearance.

In time all being ripens and its genius is displayed like those yellow leaves now soaking white the winter sun - nature's notes, necessary and sufficient. And we, though contrary and contrite, will follow those fading "few" — even me, even you.

---

[i] Author of: *Love and Will, The Courage to Create, Power and Innocence, Meaning of Anxiety, Freedom and Destiny, My Quest for Beauty.*

(*Arts Source*, December 1985)

THIEVES LIKE US

We are up to our necks in thievery! Our hearts have been stolen! So, we pursue our trespassers, our debtors, and our desire for just deserts into a new year with a resurgence of recrimination, prejudice, and pride. But before we carve out our pound of flesh, let's read again Portia's poetic defense in The Merchant of Venice, which begins: "The quality of mercy is not strained. . ."

That Shakespeare should put into the mouth of a woman one of his greatest speeches is a recognition that femininity is the goddess-source of all earthly being. Portia did have to feign masculinity if she was in a court of law) and to confound matters, women were not allowed in stage performances in Shakespeare's time. But courageously she is cast to plea for mercy.

Because awareness of this nurturing goddess-source is not alive in our culture, we do not recognize the ecological emergency of our time for the profound spiritual failure it is. Thieving and thieved upon, the world demands its pound of flesh. There is no willingness to spare,

Shylock is a man of trade; he is disciplined not to deviate. He is not a petty thief; he's too clever in calculation, too shrewd in subjugation. But he thieves, nevertheless. With a hard heart he hatefully presses for justice not knowing "that in the course of justice none of us should see salvation."

Justice is set to serve, not to save. Mercy mitigates justice: "...it is the mightiest; it becomes the throned monarch better than his crown; and earthly power doth then show likest God's when mercy seasons justice."

To resolve only to be merciful, with the magnanimity of motherhood, would certainly make for a new year, So, thieves like us must: "pray for mercy; and that same prayer doth teach us all to render the deeds of mercy."

(*Art Source*, February/March 1986)

Footnotes...

WRITERS IN RESIDENCE

If you were one of the ONE BILLION persons who viewed the Oscar presentations many Mondays ago, you saw one Oscar go to a local writer in residence (Glenn Arbor), Kurt Luedtke.

The honor of Luedtke's achievement was for best screenplay adaptation "Out of Africa". This was his second Oscar in a quick, spectacular rise out of the Hollywood hovel, the first being for his original screenplay "Absence of Malice".

It should have been noticed that the best speeches of the evening were by the veteran screenplay writer who presented Kurt Luedtke his award, Luedtke, and Barbara Streisand (a writer herself). The discipline of writing was reflected in the thoughtful selection and balance of their words.

Luedtke follows a distinguished line of writers in residence: Ernest Hemingway (Horton Bay -Walloon Lake), Robert Traver (U.P.)—"Anatomy of a Murder", Jim Harrison (Lake Leelanau)—"Farmer", and Michael Delp, poet and Director of Creative Writing at Interlochen Arts Academy. There are more writers to mention but space limits the list.

Besides their waxing of words, there is something else that ties these writers together. Harrison is releasing a new book "The Theory and Practice of Rivers and Other Poems". From his river retreat, Jim has voiced his interest in our Pigeon River (a river also once walked and written about by Hemingway). John Voelker (Traver) also knows the Pigeon and is a fancier of rivers generally—"Trout Madness", etc. Mike Delp, in his last trip to Gaylord (school workshops and

Writer's Workshop—always appreciated!), announced that he is writing a prose/poem on Steelhead fishing.

And today "The Pigeon River Country" by our own Dale Clark Franz is now in a permanent window display with these other writers at Horizon Books, Traverse City.

Rivers connect, bind, nourish. Indeed, for Northern Michigan writers, a river is a life source running through body and soul. Occasionally there will be a surfacing—of words, rare relics, remains of what is most important—a surfacing and then a going under and a moving on.

> "... he dove into an eddy catching the river's backward bend and swirl, wishing not to swim on or in as a duck and fish but to be the water herself, flowing then and still."   Jim Harrison

(Art Source, Summer 1986)

The Night Uncle Carl Caught Elk Fever

"Too cold," I told Dale. He had called to remind me that this was the time of year for our planned walk on Michigan's glorious High Country Pathway, I had never been there. "Too cold," I told him again.

Uncle Carl, he countered, is ready to drive us into the Pigeon River Forest and will pick us up when we are ready to come out. After conversation about the Great Out Doors, life passing us by, and the need for spontaneity in one's life, he finished calmly: "The Indians thought wind and cold were their friends and by exposing oneself to them, one's senses were sharpened and deepened." Why? "Because wind and cold are real!"

Dale's thrust was fatal. He had pierced to some primal need that lay dying in the bowels of my being.

As we drove into the forest, its depth and mystery began working its magic spell. Dale had the air conditioner on. I guess he was practicing, I was cold! Rounding a curve we approached an awesome sight. In the middle of the road stood the largest horned animal I had ever seen. "Look at that rack," cried Uncle Carl. "What a beautiful elk," pointing his thin quivering hand at the great bull. "Never seen anything like this, not even in Montana."

Uncle Carl had seen many animals in his long life and so I knew we were witnessing a great event. We watched the bull elk majestically stroll through a long valley. I also watched Uncle Carl's eyes fill with more than the usual amount of moisture. A man is his wettest emotion. Uncle Carl was at his ripest. "Beautiful," he kept mumbling as we drove into the camp site.

Dale had pointed out the turns to Uncle Carl as we had come in so that he would know how to get out of the forest. "Stay to your right, Uncle Carl," Dale exhorted. Uncle Carl's eyes still sparkled.

The park ranger drove us to Uncle Carl's car the next day. It was in the middle of the valley in which we had seen the great elk. Uncle Carl was gone.

I go to the Pigeon River Forest every year. I go only when it is cold. On the way in I stop at the valley and this vision occurs: I see the great elk moving proudly. Following, within fever distance, is Uncle Carl. I hear the bugle of the elk and, if I cup my ear as the Indians taught, I hear Uncle Carl's voice. The wind carries it to me through the cold and it enters my being . . . "beautiful." Then my vision begins to blur. I guess I'm coming down with elk fever too.

(*Art Source*, Spring 1987)

66

Foot Notes , . .Take the 'A' Train

You can hear the whistle blowing and see vistas beautifully and true.

To begin this wonderful journey you need go no further than downtown Gaylord. The Art Train will be on track, July 15th thru the 18th.[i]

The whistle will be the continuous hum of human activity. The vistas will be images, two dimensionally arranged, to delight the mind's eye of any seasoned traveler, it will be an excellent journey. Art and trains always provide an excellent journey. I can vouch for trains in general — that the going is still good. And I know there are many ways in which trains can serve an artistic appetite —provide vistas beautiful and true. Another example: since trains will take you to the center of most cities, art museums (as well as other cultural sights) become more accessible, I boarded the 'A' train in Detroit last February. It took me to Chicago, Dallas, Fort Worth, Orlando, St. Petersburg, Washington D.C., New York City, Montreal and back to Detroit, I visited one or more museums in every city mentioned.

There is too much to say about all of this for one reading but one point can be made, one example given: The great art of the world is so spread out that I now realize more than ever the necessity for traveling exhibitions and retrospective shows. The major cities do not always have the major artist — Dallas is, in this respect, more impoverished than Flint; and some obscure town in Georgia (the name of which I can't even remember) now is the home of one of the great collections in America due to a private bequeath! I found America's greatest painter {and one of my favorite paintings) in the Fort Worth Museum that owns few other great masters: "The Swimming Hole" by Thomas Eakins (which adorns the Penguin edition of Walt Whitman's poetry collection).

So, take the 'A' train — take it first to Gaylord — then take it around the world. The whistle says that the going is still good, that the vistas are still beautiful and true.

---

[i] Made possible by an endowment from the Gornick Fund.

(*Art Source*, Summer 1987)

A Commentary:

On *The Closing of the American Mind*
Winter Work

"Standing on the snow-covered plain, as if in a pasture amid the hills, I cut my way first through a foot of snow, and then a foot of ice, and open a window under my feet, where, kneeling to drink, I look down into the quiet parlor of the fishes, pervaded by a softened light as through a window of ground glass, with its bright sanded floor the same as in summer; there a perennial waveless serenity reigns as in the amber twilight sky, corresponding to the cool and even temperment of the inhabitants. Heaven is under our feet as well as over our heads."

Such light is the product of Thoreau's afternoon work. In the morning he would spend time reading, thawing out an inner resource also frozen over "after a still winter night." This, of course, produced more light.

For Allan Bloom, author of this year's most talked-about book, this freezing over has become permanent in our modern world. It will take more than Thoreau's axe and a few winter mornings to reverse *The Closing of the American Mind.*

But it is heartwarming that such a book (which could have been more clearly written without lessening the profundity of its ideas — like Walden) has stayed as long as it has at the top of the best seller list. That liberal arts and the humanities should be the forefront and content of higher education places Bloom's book among the other fine defenses of this noble position. More warmth!

But there is a warning: "liberals" will not find an ally here — The Closing *of the* American Mind is most "conservative." The vaunted concerns of the 1960's were nothing more than "evanescent mist" —"high intellectual life became inextricably linked with American barbarism." And furthermore "the gutter phenomenon of rock ruins the imagination." Bloom's academic background of political science seems to give him a reactionary penchant. A most temporary (but timely) image of a Bork in Bloom helps, both ways, to a further understanding.

But at the bottom of Allen Bloom's book, as in Henry Thoreau's pond, there reigns great issues that are most bright, and an opening is given for a perennial view, the content of which is more than enough for winter work.

(*Art Source*, Winter 1988)

A More Stately Manner

From time to time we are informed by one medium or another that some aspiring person to some respected position is or is not "to the manor born." (Dan Quayle is a recent example.)

To be of "the manor" in this context denotes a class aristocratic and privileged in the Old World and plutocratic and positioned in the New World. In accepting this demarcation, one might labor life-long under tinges of envy and imagined injustices resulting in feelings of resentment; or if under the illusion of being one of the chosen few, to suffer the same though from feelings of insecurity (masked by arrogance) and guilt (repressed by diversion).

But what do we find when we look to the source of this often quoted phrase? Shakespeare's Hamlet begins: "But to my mind, though I am native here, and to the manner born..." Manner (custom, habit, mode of behavior) not "manor" is the correct word and even *Webster's New International Dictionary, 2nd Ed.*, comments on this most common of errors. Though Hamlet is a prince and Shakespeare is a master of the witty pun, both are believers in a manner of mind that becomes a source of wealth. Furthermore, the seriousness of the context (why some men drink too much) supports the larger, richer, more resonant "manner."

Hamlet assigns to the mind the highest authority — those prerogatives of customs — manners indigenous to each new born. These 'rights' are introduced to us in a tradition of guidance and then continue in us through a tradition of transcendence. They are universal — discipline to freedom.

To commit ourselves (thus compounding the error)

to the lesser reality of the "manor" really is to relinquish our birth right and all that widening potentiality that follows — that we are by human nature inheritors of a unique mental capacity and are by native right progenitors of a human conduct, a way of doing and speaking, the manner of which is responsive, respectful, and resourceful.

It is a manner so self-evident that it holds us to its mandate like the highest law — even though, Hamlet continues, it is "sometimes more honored in the breach than the observance."

When man's mind functions as man's mind, that man comes into man's estate. As human beings, from our beginning equally and equally to our end, we are all, in fact, "to the manner born."

(*Art Source*, Winter 1989)

Poet As Critic

"His (the poet's) brain is the ultimate brain. . .he is judgement. . .he is complete in himself."

Walt Whitman, Preface to *Leaves of Grass*.

Since life is short and its redeemer art long, I find the views of Joseph Brodsky, who was awarded the 1987 Nobel Prize in Literature, of the utmost importance. In "How to Read a Book" (*N. Y. Times Book Review*, June 12, 1988) Brodsky commiserates with our moribund condition, but only if "I've read not for reading's sake, but to learn. Hence, the need for concision, condensation, fusion — "for works that bring the human predicament, in all its diversity, into its sharpest possible focus." Hence, the need for a solution — a short cut not only for reading but a method of learning for writing also.

What is the "only" solution that Brodsky offers that would serve as a guide, compass, and filter for developing a sound taste in literature? Reviews and criticisms he rules out for being unreliable, too restricted, or if cultivated and informed, too long (we won't get to the work itself). To develop good taste in literature one must read poetry!

Poetry is supreme because being concise it conveys in the most condensed way the human condition. All those disciplines which produce the highest possible standards for writing and reading are guaranteed. "The more one reads poetry, the less tolerant one becomes of verbosity. . . good style is always hostage to the precision, speed and laconic intensity of poetic diction. Above all, poetry develops in prose that appetite for metaphysics that distinguishes a work of art from mere belle lettres."

Economy, value, mental dexterity, emphasis to detail and technique all make poetry a self-contained authority.

Brodsky concludes that this armed vision is obtained in a matter of months from the works of poets in your mother tongue preferably from the first half of this century. In English he recommends: Robert Frost, Thomas Hardy, W. B. Yeats, T. S. Eliot, W. H. Auden, Marianne Moore and Elizabeth Bishop. Each body of work is thinner in pages than that neon Gothic pulp you quickly grabbed at the last airport.

This is good news to readers and writers who have been wandering in limbo, undirected and without discernment, their only absolute being ruinous time. For salvation is to be found amongst pearls of poetry that deliver pure prose (poetry); and like Beatrice unto Dante in paradise forever guiding, so poetry unto poetry guides us — forever upward.

(*Art Source*, Spring/Summer 1989)

Sit and Deliver!

The act of artistic creation, making something out of nothing, is born in fear (risk), is pursued in power (control), and results in joy (relief).

The great command to our fleeting spirit is: Deliver! With this artistic deliverance, false starts, renewed promises, all plans in fact, are mocked and silenced. When we deliver a creative effort we consummate, however rhetorical or imitative, a commitment to our deepest concern fulfilling our deepest need: communication.

If your way is writing then you must sit and deliver -and sources for inspiration are ever at hand. A whimsical little ditty was recently presented[1] by the "Titanic" author, Robert Stone *(Dog Soldiers,* movie: *Who'll Stop the Rain; A Flag at Sunrise; Children of Light).* In *The Reason for Stories* he argues for a moral fiction and states that what follows "may contain the essence of every work of serious literature ever written." It certainly contains the great command and why the creative act consumes so much passion and time. "Of offering more than what we can deliver, we have a bad habit it is true. "But we have to offer more than what we can deliver to be able to deliver what we do."[2]

---

[1] *Harper's Magazine*, June 1988.

[2] From *Letters from Leelanau.* Kathleen Stocking received the 10th Annual Bay de Noc Writers' Conference Best Emerging Writer Award in 1989. She is working on a second book of essays called Lake Country.

(*Art Source*, Spring 1990)

The Music Of An Unsung Hero

The man that hath no music in himself,
Nor is not moved with concord of sweet sounds,
Is fit for treasures, stratagems and spoils;
The motions of his spirit are dull as night,
And his affections dark as Erebus.
Let no such man be trusted. Mark the music.
Wm. Shakespeare, The Merchant of Venice

The old cliche and renowned understatement of the teacher as undervalued, underpaid—the unsung hero in a society that prizes achievements other than a good education for its people—was nevertheless as true in my youth as it is today. Our education policy throws everything at an institution (including money) in the futile hope that illiteracy and crime can be held in abeyance while raising the educational level of the general populace. Only with a revolution in consciousness respecting education and the teacher's role in society will any significant change occur.

The above thoughts were visited upon me recently as I sat listening to an orchestral and choral concert at the Eglise de la Madeleine in Paris, France. Moved by the pleading strains of Mozart's Requiem (preceded poignantly by Shubert's Unfinished Symphony – *Symphonie Inachievie*) I pondered the fate of the unsung hero of my youth. His name was Ralph Deal and he taught 10th grade civics. Ralph Deal was an educated man: impeccable in speech, erudite in thought, eloquent in delivery. He epitomized the classic proposition: an educated man is a rich man. Ralph Deal was a rich man.

The male models of our community were hard boiled executives who thought they knew how to manufacture and market automobiles (and related products) and little else. They were honored like heroes. By contrast, Ralph Deal was not only rumoured to be "light in his loafers," but, because he was working on another master's degree in Russian language, we hung upon him the equally opprobrious nickname, "Red Ralph" (this was the time of the infamous McCarthy hearings). All of this produced gigglings of gossip, false witnessing, and cruelty (always behind Mr. Deal's back—what gutless wonders we were).

A student was required to take and pass civics. Mr. Deal announced early in the year of his course that he was conducting a voluntary two hour per week, unaccredited music appreciation study. What better way than this, a group of us calculated, to influence one's way to a passing grade in civics. Over the year, Mr. Deal would guide us through recordings of such musical compositions as Tchaikovsky's Fifth, Beethoven's Fifth, Seventh, & Ninth, Dvorak's New World, Rachmaninoff's 2nd Piano Concerto, and Stravinsky's Rite of Spring. We would then, under his supervision, attend live performances of the Detroit Symphony Orchestra seeing and hearing what we had previously studied.

Mr. Deal continued to conduct his music appreciation course as an extra curricular activity and eventually he taught Russian. I'm sure he influenced many students. But I was aware that beneath this positive surface was a suffering that surely was not due to his alleged "lightness" or "Redness." I surmised this in our conversations at the University of Michigan where he pursued his additional master's degree and in his face that I glimpsed later as he wandered the high school neighborhood, "retired" before his time.

We do not know ultimately what forces effect the agony of a mind or the suffering of a soul but from my perspective, Mr. Deal, a man of talent and cultured sensitivity, endured loneliness, misunderstanding (or worse—non-under-standing), low esteem all those casual indifferences that our society offers to a declining educational system. (A recent study claims that the trend has been reversed to 1970 standards, the base year being anywhere from 1965 back to the 1930's depending who is doing the judging. With television and the computer entering the classroom, the 1970 standards are likely to look, if not archaic, then very good in the near future.)

After high school, I went on to ply the musical influence of Mr. Deal. Between Detroit and Ann Arbor I was able during college years to see in person: Maria Callas, Rinalda Tibaldi, Isaac Stern, Rudolph Serkin, Eugene Ormandy, Leonard Bernstein and Herbert Von Karajan.

This was followed with three years in New York City. In person: Leontyne Price, Joan Sutherland, more Callas (you know Maria Callas from the recent movie Philadelphia). All of this was capped by serving as an extra in two Metropolitan Opera productions featuring Briget Nielson — Pucini's Tosca and Verdi's Aida.

These musings in homage to Mr. Deal, as I said, were given incubation at the majestic Madeleine in Paris, as the Orchestre Symphonique Ama-Deus and the Ensemble Polyphonique de Versailles worked their way through the "Lacrimosa" (oh, this day full of tears) section of Mozart's Requiem. At this point, I may have experienced what is known in Greek tradegy and explained by Aristotle as the purging of the emotions by art — a carthartic release. You know the "Lacrimosa" movement. It is played in that part of the movie "Amadeus" when the grave attendants deliver Mozart's body to a common pit, dump it in, shovel lime over it in preparation for the next body. Or maybe I was just experiencing one of Linda Richman's "verklemmts".

A week later, I attended, at the beautiful Opera De Paris Garnier, a tribute to Nijinski, the renown ballet dancer and choreographer. The program with full orchestra and ballet were selections from Strauss' *Till Eulenspiegel*, Stravinsky's *Petrouchka*, and a major portion of his *Rite of Spring* — *Le Sacre Du Printemps*.

I have never been a fan of ballet, but, with all the color and action on stage in this most elegant 19th century opera house interior, it was a gorgeous visual feast. Still, for me, the joy of the evening was not the dancing but the music and for all I cared, they were not honoring Nijinski, but Mr. Deal.

Stravinsky's Rite of Spring centers Walt Disney's animated film classic *Fantasia* (1939).[1] It is also one of the acknowledged cultural symbols for the rise of modernism in the 20th century.[2] The Rite of Spring received five curtain calls that evening. I was thrilled to be hearing and seeing this performance in Paris, not only because of all the above, but doubly for the ironic fact (as I was once told) that this performance met with such furor when it was first introduced in 1913 in this very same city. I was once told— no—I was once taught this forty-some years ago. Mark the music. Mark the man.

---

[1] The late French horn player, James Stagliano, a summer resident here in Gaylord, told me that he performed for Leopold Stowkowski in this production of "Fantasia." Stagliano played under the famous Serge Koussevitzky, conductor of the Boston Symphony Orchestra, for 25 years and thus knew every great composer of the 20th century. Richard Strauss made a special trip to the U.S. to hear Stagliano introduce his 2nd Horn Concerto to the American public. Stagliano amused me with his observations of Stravinsky's obsession with hardware stores – a possible insight into his music. Also amusing were stories of his late night libations with Ferdi Grofe (Grand Canyon, Mississippi Suites) who he felt

was underrated as he felt Aaron Copland (*Appalachian Spring, Rodeo*) was overrated.

² *Rites of Spring: The Great War and The Birth of The Modern Age* by Modris Eksteins (1990) is only the latest indication of this acknowledgment.

(*Art Source*, Winter 1995)

HAMLET AND HAMM: THEIR FINAL ANSWER

"The readiness is all." Hamlet
(*Hamlet*, William Shakespeare, 1600)

"Ah the old questions, the old answers, there's nothing like them."
Hamm (*Endgame*, Samuel Beckett, 1957)

A specter is haunting the world: the specter of death—the death of reading.

This thought evolves out of a recent discussion: whether the use of computers will lead to a greater degree of literacy. On one side you have the proponents that claim people are not reading, that the computer gets people reading, that the computer will be the leading writing tool and reading source for the future. This is, in part, represented by the facile imaginings of Andrew Sullivan who, in his *New York Times Magazine* article, "Dot-communism Manifesto" (6-11-00), sees the computer as the mind's liberation from the marketing machinations of capitalism and the disciplinary controls of tradition.

But there are those who feel that the computer will only further diminish already diminishing reading, communicative skills. This is represented by extending T. S. Eliot's famous dictum: "Where is the wisdom lost in knowledge? Where is the knowledge lost in information?" with the further question: Where is the information lost in data? "Data" is fragments, incomplete sentences, poor syntax, no punctuation, no sense.

I use to be a proponent of the adage that any kind of reading, particularly at the beginning of one's education, was better than no reading. But, for me, the computer puts an end to that idea: Woe unto the wasteland within our schools.

There are a myriad of reasons why this death is happening but happening it is and, for me, the specter of Nothingness that haunts Hamlet and Hamm finds its approximation and continuation, though diminutively and less nobly, in the computer. I will explore this further but first let's hear what is passing, what is past.

In a New Yorker magazine interview (5-8-00) the renown American author, Phillip Roth talks about "the death of reading." He first points to the evidence that the literary era has come to an end: culture and society are now reflected on the screen - movie, television and now the computer screen. No longer do we have the time, habits of mind, silence, and concentration to pursue literature. He then talks about the intellectual and artistic effort, "the great mission to explore consciousness" in the first half of the 20th century. It was an effort to "see behind things" and this is now of no interest, because there has been a narrowing of consciousness. He talks about this great mission being pursued. by, among others, Freud, Joyce, Kafka, Marx, Proust, and Beckett. "By the death of reading I mean that this great human endeavor has come to an end. Believe me, I know."

Another judgment is from Cynthia Ozick, essayist and scholar, in a *New York Times Magazine* (5-7-00) article titled "Where to Connect to The Inner Hum-Turnoff, Tune Out: Read a Novel." Generally, Ozick feels that the electronic media, while appearing to be personal, individual, and open to interpretation, is in reality the concealed machinations of mass psychology, closed and absolute.

Her great and original insight is that the enemy of the inner life is the crowd. She describes inner life as discernment, penetration, imagination, self-knowledge. The mind is "many-threaded, mazy, meandering and murmuring" while every crowd is merely or mainly a machine. "Contemporary story-grinding contrivances and appliances that purport to capture the inner life—what are they, really, if not the brute extrusions of the principle of Crowds?" She includes, on her list of crowd producing contrivances, films with their rolling credits, television with its newsy happy talk and talk-show confessionals, radio talk show psychology, "the retrograde e-mail contagion that reduces letter writing to stunted 19th-century telegraphese," electronic chat rooms and magazines (those that misleadingly pass as reading material) that "debase discourse" with their "hollow breeziness" and their nonstop pursuit of the "cutting edge." Again - "what are they, really, if not the dwarfing gyrations of crowds? Chat is not an essay; film is not a novel. The micro-universe of the modem? Never mind." Ozick ends her essay saying the inner life eludes these multiplying high-tech implements: "The inward hum of fragility, hope, transcendence, dread—where in an age of machines addressing crowds, and crowds mad for machines, can it be found? In the art of the novel; in its infinity of plasticity and elasticity. And nowhere else." So where does all this leave us? In one of those "Best of the Century -Millennium" lists that in updated publications toward the end of the 20th-century, the *New York Times Magazine* (4-18-99) supplied some of the most insightful contributions. Among them was the selection of William Shakespeare's Hamlet, by Harvard's Helen Vendler (*The Art of Shakespeare's Sonnets*, 1997), as the greatest poem (emphasizing the lyrical over the dramatic) of the Millennium—"our pre-eminent post-Christian poem." The lyrical Hamlet with his infinite consciousness is only moved by death (not revenge) and in repudiating consolation provides the philosophical turning point for the last millennium in the West. All authority, both regal and religious, henceforth begins to collapse—"The readiness is all."

From Hamlet to Hamm, Samuel Beckett's enduring character from his masterpiece, *Endgame*, we have the final winding down of two grand traditions. Harold Bloom ends his *The Western Canon* (1994) with the idea that the play *Endgame*, "The Hamlet of our elegiac era," ends the Canon: "literature's last stand." We are amidst another sea change certainly not unrelated to an earlier one—the solidification of the secular over the sacred (the sacred and secular of a tradition when they were not merely political and social determinations)—"Ah the old questions, the old answers"— labeled "post-Christian" in Hamlet's and our brave new world.

Now we are experiencing the solidification of the computer over the book(s)—"there's nothing like them"— now searching for a label — post-traditional education—of how and what we learn in Hamm's and our brave new world of not diminished but redirected consciousness and not denied but redirected transcendence. Again, tradition being authoritative, all that which was considered important in book form is now eroding as a new world emerges.

From Hamlet to Hamm the loss is sealed, that both Roth and Ozick lament. For good or bad, the secular trend that begins with Hamlet's lyrical imaginings reaches its zenith with Hamm's poetic finalities in what may be the last of the literary. The computer is the ultimate symbol for this secular spirit. Beckett doesn't allude to Hamlet himself— Hamm is taken from the name of the biblical Noah's surviving son (significant in itself)—but we cannot fail to see the alliterative and especially the philosophical connection between the two characters. This theme of loss is a continuation of Beckett's most famous play *Waiting for Godot* (1954), perhaps the most succinct and pithy title of modern times for the human condition—again the unacknowledged allusion to God is obvious. Both Hamlet and Hamm, being the great representatives of lost and found, present the final threnody—their immortal lamentations that symbolically memorialize our fate. With Hamlet and Hamm, we have found our future.

Undoubtedly this conclusion produces a reflective skepticism but not necessarily pessimism or nihilism, both products of self-absorption. While we live, there is no endgame; there is only hope. As with Christians in their catacombs (1st century), so it is with readers in their libraries—both marginal societies buffered from a sometimes cruel and crude world. As Beckett says, we are between a death and a difficult birth. But we need not hold to another's despair, another's optimism—not yet.

Peace comes with tolerance and faith, hope, and charity merge with the secular. As human beings, our only obligation, from which all else follows, is to have courage, seek beauty, and show joy.

(Art Source, 2001)

The Prince, The Pauper, and The Pragmatist

The word turns. The word turns and the knower in his turn reads again something new, rich, and imaginative. The word turns and to know how and why requires continuous and close reading. The word turns and everyday evidence evinces from me the indictment: If you don't read, you don't know!

The word "prince" is attached to Shakespeare's Hamlet, perhaps the greatest literary personality ever. Shakespeare, himself, teaches that the word turns, "sets word against word." Hamlet is the Prince of Denmark, heir to the King's throne and his Kingdom. But he is also the prince and progenitor of man's mind not, as Nietzsche said, because he thinks too much, but because he thinks too well Even so, Hamlet says of himself, that he is "to the manner born," to a common state of existence. "Manner" (custom, habit, mode of behavior) not "manor" is the correct word and *Webster's New International Dictionary, 2nd Ed.*, points up this most common error. Though Hamlet is a prince and Shakespeare a master of the witty pun, both are, in this context and generally, believers in a manner of mind that is the true source of wealth and the highest authority. This is the only "manor" to which we are born. To commit oneself to the "manor" (which Prince Hamlet does not) at the expense of the "manner" is to err twice!

Thus Hamlet's princely and poetic meditations on the human condition (thus making paupers of us all) have elicited grand accolades: Harvard University's Helen Vendler, among others, thinks *Hamlet*, considered lyrically, is the greatest poem of the last millennium, our "pre-eminent 'post-Christian' poem." The English critic, Sir Frank Kermode calls *Hamlet* the "poem unlimited" borrowing the phrase from the play's own

Polonius, and that it is "literatures greatest bazaar" (*Shakespeare's Language*, 2000). Yale University's Harold Bloom says that Hamlet is "the fiercest inwardness (and the most intelligent character) ever achieved in a literary work" (*Shakespeare: The Invention of the Human*, 1988).

The word "pauper", conversely, can be applied by background, to Abraham Lincoln, one of our greatest presidents. Yet Lincoln was truly to the "manor" born, that being the White House in our nation's capital.

Lincoln, democracy's champion, had a life-long contempt, probably born of his own low entry into life, for the idea that accidents of rank (such as that of a prince) imply a hierarchy of intrinsic worth. We are achieving Lincoln's America where exclusivity, when it is not pure fantasy, will remain ineffectively private for, as Henry David Thoreau knew: "To enjoy a thing exclusively is commonly to exclude yourself from the true enjoyment of it."

Hamlet works pragmatically to avenge his father's premeditated death while he believes only in death. For him God is death. . . "the undiscovered country from whose bourne no traveler returns." Reality for Hamlet, like those Gnostics who intuit a deeper knowledge—is his "knowing" that "the readiness is all....the rest is silence." Harold Bloom says that Hamlet is one of the few ambassadors sent by death to us who does not lie about our future journey and that it is also inevitably solitary "despite all of tradition's obscene attempts to socialize it" (*The Western Canon, The Book and School of the Ages,* 1994). Only Lincoln's poet, the American Walt Whitman, fully celebrates this Gnostic God/Death reality in such an exultant manner as Shakespeare.

Even so, Hamlet's Gnostic self-reliance is in detail, best represented, by Lincoln's intellectual contemporary, Ralph Waldo Emerson. Emerson is the prophet of a new Gnosticism that is now permeating the American religious imagination "whether it is Protestant, Catholic, Judaic, Islamic, Buddhist, Hindu or secular, whether it is known or not." This "American religion" is an original blending of Emerson's self-reliant "knowing" ("I am part and parcel of God") with the philosophic freedom and power of his new pragmatism: "Life only avails, not the having lived. Power ceases in the instant of repose; it resides in the moment of transition. . . ." (Self Reliance) How Emerson's American Gnosticism gives us the freedom to pursue his American philosophy of pragmatism, undermining criticism of righteousness and relativism, will have to be saved for a later essay.

Lincoln works pragmatically to save the Union from death and does not let even God get in the way: Fearing that the state of Kentucky might secede from the Union (thus diminishing drastically the North's railroad network), Lincoln supported Kentucky's position as a slave state. An irate woman approached him: "Mr. President, God is not happy with you." Lincoln replied, "I'm sorry to make God unhappy, madam, but I need Kentucky to win the war" (proving Lincoln a humorist and a military strategist).

Hamlet had many detractors: Polonius, Rosencrantz and Gildenstern, Claudius, and Laertes. Lincoln, though it seems that he had many, really had only one: the aristocratic, arrogant George McCellan. Hamlet rids his detractors with a sword; Lincoln rids his with Grant and Sherman. Hamlet is known as the melancholy prince. Lincoln, according to his friend and law partner, William Herndon, "dripped with melancholy." They both, with equal courage, looked into the abyss for help and saw nothing. But they both were pragmatists and got the job done without those real "hells" that usually attend "good intentions" — righteousness, rationalization, theory, abstraction, and

88

ideology.

Both Hamlet and Lincoln are memorialized by the written word "so ambiguous in intent yet so rich in future imaginings" by Shakespeare's play and Lincoln's own letters and speeches. The writing of the first is generally acknowledged the greatest in world literature, the height of intellect and imagination; the writing of the second, in the view of one American critic, among others, Stanley Edgar Hyman, is "with the possible exception of Henry David Thoreau, the only first-rate prose ever written by an American."

Hamlet and Lincoln, interchangeably the prince and the pauper, are both pragmatist: Crowned consciousness of cares and causes, centerless and contingent, coping, communing.

(Art Source, 2001-02)

AMERICA THE SUBLIME

Traveling is a serendipitous affair. This was made apparent to me again when I revisited the *Musee D'Orsay* this year in Paris. There was a longer than usual line out side, down the block and around the corner. To my surprise (I never inquired ahead) there was an exhibit of the American painter, Thomas Eakins (1844-1916). This was the first retrospective of Eakins I had ever seen — so many paintings, drawn from many museums and private art collections from all around the United States, all under one roof.

Eakins is regarded, by most critics, to be the greatest of American realist painters — our American Rembrandt. Of special interest to me was the portrait of Walt Whitman who sat for Eakins. It adorns many collections of Whitman's poetry and criticism and therefore I knew it existed but had never seen it. Surely this was pure serendipity for one American in Paris.

In London, on the same trip, another surprise awaited me. At the Tate Britain (to distinguish it now from the new Tate Modern across the Thames where another American was being exhibited, Andy Warhol, now in Los Angeles, CA for the summer) there was a monumental exhibition; *American Sublime: Landscape Paintings in the United States, 1820-1880*. In eight rooms, hung over ninety paintings, all oils, mainly from the Hudson River School including Thomas Cole, Asher Durand, John Frederik Kensett, Thomas Moran, Frederik Edwin Church, and Albert Bierstadt. These artists were inspired by the huge range and splendor of the American landscape: The Hudson River Valley, the Niagara Falls, the Rocky Mountains, the Grand Canyon, the Yellowstone and Yosemite Valleys. I doubt that there had ever been an exhibition of this size and importance anywhere in the United States. Again of particular interest was that on the cover of the catalogue handed to all viewers was a Frederick Edwin Church sunset loaned by the Detroit Institute of Arts. Thomas Moran's first American journey was to the shores of Lake Superior in 1861.

This was the inspiration for three paintings exhibited on Longfellow's poem *The Song of Hiawatha* that also celebrates the shores of Lake Superior. And finally, there were two paintings (Kensett and Gifford) on loan from Detroit's Manoogian collection, one of the great private collections of American art, a part of which can be seen in rotation at the Grand Hotel on Mackinac Island.

Serendipity had struck again and, for me, paradise had been regained. The exhibition was no less than awesome, a word I seldom use, reserving it for the splendid overpowering grandeurs of nature. Awesome is a trendy word usually used by young people who don't know or appreciate its resonant, profound meaning. (My eight year old grandson uses it all the time).

More difficult to understand is the lovely but vague notion of "the sublime". The Tate Britain, in an understandably English tribute, declares to the viewer that these paintings can be seen as the ultimate expressions of the eighteenth-century aesthetic concept of the sublime — defined by the English thinker Edmund Burke as an effect productive of the strongest emotion the mind is capable of feeling. This is an accurate application as far as it goes. However, as an American, I think that the American Sublime has been ultimately defined by the founding American thinkers: Emerson, Thoreau, and Whitman. This has been a major theme, for me, as expressed particularly in part II (1997-98) of "The Declaration of America: American Aesthetes, Regal Readers", *Art Source,* Otsego County Library, Gaylord, MI.

Yale University's Harold Bloom, in his chapters

"Emerson: The American Religion" and "Whitman's Image of Voice" (*Agon,* Oxford Press, 1982) states that of the three American thinkers, Emerson is the primary and initial representative of the American Sublime and that Whitman, because "he *is* voice in our poetry, quite simply *is* the American Sublime". To this I have added that Thoreau is the prose proponent of the American Sublime.

This concept of the "American Sublime" is original with Bloom, his mixture of democracy, gnosticism, aestheticism, and pragmatism — the American difference that in both exhibits, Paris and London, in a time of imperial prerogatives and pretensions, places Sublime America over Pax Americana. However one understands the word "sublime"; walking thorough this vast exhibit is a start that surely will acquaint one with any and all feelings and meanings that any and all definitions could supply.

How did the English receive the exhibit? Like Eakins in Paris, the reception started with long lines. Here is one English reviewer's response: "I have seen a few over-the-top sunsets in art in my time, I have seen Turner (J.M.W. Turner — England's greatest impressionist painter and one given the most permanent space at the Tate Britain) at his most genuflectory, but I have never seen anything quite as orgiastically red and delirious as Church's "Twilight in the Wilderness".. . I would rate this as one of the most exciting and revelatory exhibitions I have seen in recent years". Waldemar Januszczak, *London Sunday Times,* 2-08-02. Traveling is a serendipitous affair. After London, *American Sublime* was exhibited at the Pennsylvania Academy of the Fine Arts, in Philadelphia. It will be at the Minneapolis Institute of Arts, September 22 to November 17, 2002. I have no further dates for either exhibit but trust to a sublime serendipity that interested viewers and this awe inspiring art shall meet.   (*Art Source,* 2002)

Part III

Book Reviews and Prefaces

"There are no adventures like intellectual ones."
(Henry James)

Book Review

Evil & Evolution: A Theodicy[1]

> *"I am bound upon a wheel of fire
> that my own tears do scald like molten
> lead."*
>
> King Lear

The problem of suffering is one of the most important and interesting issues of religious thought. That it should be the topic of the second book by a Catholic theologian who lives in the wilds of northern Michigan near Gaylord also points up its universality.

A theodicy is an attempt to justify God's ways to man. Fr. Kropf shows in *Evil and Evolution: A Theodicy* how this problem has been wrestled with by all faiths in all times: Job in the Old Testament, St. Augustine in his "City of God," Luther in his protest, Carnus in his existential novels, and Teilhard de Chardin (French Catholic) in his recent evolutionary writings (from whom Kropf takes his lead).

In addition, Kropf effectively uses classic literary sources (Dostoyevsky's *The Brothers Karamazov* being the most powerful) to keep the problem of evil on a human and understandable level.

God's justice, power, goodness, and man's freedom and will are at the center of this theodicy. With sensitivity and concern, Kropf diffuses, but does not entirely solve, the problems of evil by applying the understanding of evolutionary thought.

But man's responsibility is never absolved; "Freedom consists not in the wiping out of the past, but in its

96

utilization, and in the transformation of the chance influences of the past into material for new, conscious, self-determination." Nor is mystery, faith, and transcendence denied. And the challenge and struggle continues: "it is a battle of quality versus quantity, over whether there is to be a better future for the human race or simply more of the same."

There is in the writings of Fr. Kropf an evolutionary "Convergence" of his own concentrated and concerned thought. He approaches the problem of evil in the full dress of modernity; participation, challenge-struggle, and change. But his disciplined mind will not allow for easy answers, only vital choices — and an unbounding transcendence.

[1] Author: Richard W. Kropf; Fairleigh Dickinson University Press, 1984.

(*Arts Source,* Fall 1986)

Review

Walking and Golf[1]

Walking is a complimentary activity to many sports. It serves as an exercise leading up to the sport. It serves as a relaxation winding down from the sport. Walking can also be the threading action from beginning to end providing the above services and more. Golf comes to mind as the sport that most perfectly embodies this energetic activity of walking.

Traditionally the walking involved in playing golf was a good part of the joy produced by the game. My own impressions and those of friends when talking of golf is how a certain golf course remains in the memory—its length, layout, condition of terrain, size of hills, density of trees, amount of water, etc. - the combination of which would be discussed in glowing terms impressing upon one's mind a picture of grand and stately beauty. And for most, these impressions were gained and remain more through walking that course than on a particular occasion in which an unusually low score or a most difficult putt was achieved.

If walking while playing golf, a natural setting is generally agreed upon to be one of the great attractions of the game. There is another level in which walking particularly adds to the quality of the game of golf itself. A person walking on and through a golf course becomes externally and internally (consciously and un-consciously) a unique instrument (with feeling) of measurement.

Externally, one sizes up (measures) the day—temperature, wind, humidity, light. A golfer, because he is on foot and out in the open, continuously absorbs the elements and makes mental calculations even as they imperceptibly change throughout the game. In applying these measurements hole by hole the golfer is not unlike the most exacting scientist.

The golfer also has gained two great advantages given to walkers: an accurate lay of the land and a discerning judgement of distance. By walking, one most naturally extends oneself into the surrounding environment, partaking of its influences, recording onto oneself the shape and measure of this world. By repetition this process comes to be known as experience. And this experience becomes part of one's self knowledge, intuitions that strike deep roots allowing the golfer to perfect his game because he knows. It becomes a physical and mental accomplishment as fulfilling as the executions of a good drive or perfect putt.

Internally, the walking golfer takes careful measure-ment of himself—works up then works down, reflects then relaxes interchangeably throughout the game. First, mind and body, already conditioned, approach and work through a challenging problem (ball, shot, play). Then there is a relaxing and reflecting as one walks to the next problem, again to be worked through. Optimum attention has been worked up and now the attending stress is worked (walked) down. With the interaction of reflection and relaxation, this mental and physical process is allowed to revitalize and ready itself as one walks to the next problem. The activity of golf is supported and thus enhanced by the activity of walking.

This most natural ability to take and give measurement in one's walk through a golf course is really more miraculous than all the technologies that have come to surround the game. Miraculous and yet most understandable since the human being is allowed to interact naturally with his or her surroundings. This is as it should be. And the game of golf, itself, becomes one way in which we receive a glimpse of this living process.

The golfer, through walking, has become one with the earthly elements, thus creating a source—always available— of power and perfection, of health and excellence, of confidence and joy.

---

[1] An essay inspired by *A Tribute to Golf, A Celebration in Art, Photography and Literature*, by Thomas P. Stewart.

(Art Source,Winter 1990)

Review

FANTASTIC NEWS[1]

Could a greater miracle take place than for us to look through each other's eyes for an instant? (Walden)

On the trail of Henry David Thoreau, I came across some years ago a critical study by Stanley Cavell, Harvard University professor of philosophy and asethetics, called *The Senses of Walden* (1981). This study goes well beyond those that only look at the naturalist, the economist, the rebel, the humourist, etc. in Thoreau — positions that are easily reduced, out of context, into those pithy and profound quotations that adorn Sierra Club calendars, nature documentaries made for television (and book reviews). But Cavell as critic leads properly back to Thoreau and therefore would have been shelved as a personal passing interest if it were not for a review that led me to his most recent work, *The Quest For The Ordinary* (1990). Here, in this book, I did find something new, something worth passing on, something even "fantastic" as Cavell himself would claim.

"Thoreau's *Walden* is the major philosophic text of my life—other than Wittgenstein's *Philosophical Investigations*." This is Cavell's opening statement in a book that is a collection of lectures given at the universities of Stanford, Harvard, and Vienna. For Cavell, Emerson and Thoreau are the founding thinkers of American culture. They underwrite his mentors Ludwig Wittgenstein and J. C. Austin—progenitors of the twentieth century movement called ordinary language philosophy which is related to analytical and positivistic philosophy. For Cavell, Emerson and Thoreau contribute "a romantic taint" and compliment "what I regard as some of the most advanced thought of our time." And this is the romantic (because of its transcendental faith) demand for redemption — self-recovery — philosophy's essential business being a response and recovery from skepticism (the modern condition for Cavell). This is the recovery, quest — of our ordinary voice — of the everyday — of common life.

Cavell believes that literature is the transcendentalizing of the domestic and in addition, particularly with Emerson and Thoreau, a democratizing of philosophy thus linking the transcendentalism of Kant and Coleridge through Emerson and Thoreau to Heidegger and Holderlin. This is then the enlisting of Emerson and Thoreau in the business of ordinary language philosophy, bringing them into the Modem Movement according to Cavell "to word the world together" with reading and writing that redeems. This is a noble effort by Cavell (and others) to democratize the whole literary and philosophic enterprise. After all, ordinary language is that of communion and community and this is the language that binds us to the world that is also the world of others.

In the writings of Emerson and Thoreau, Americanism and democracy are one and paramount: a rooted conviction that the world must be open to all, that natural language and tongues of nature spoken therein are those of the colloquial. The philosophic impulse, the literary exercise and the delights that they nurture are not to be the secret and exclusive pursuits of mandarins but belong to the shared hunger for "the conversion of the world" (Emerson) which has been the very hallmark of American destiny and democratic communion, the literary and philosophic foundation being supplied by Emerson and Thoreau.

This is indeed, for me, welcome news and such recognition, delayed as it is, would warrant from me the accolade "fantastic," but not from Stanley Cavell. Not yet.

The final lecture in Cavell's book is titled: "The Fantastic of Philosophy" and was delivered at a Wittgenstein celebration at the Philosophical Institute of the University of Vienna. Cavell opens: "The interest among philosophers here in the richness of specifically Austrian thought has helped my own preoccupation with the richness and the poverty of specifically American thought, above all with the extraordinary fact that those I regard as the founders of American thinking—Ralph Waldo Emerson and Henry David Thoreau—are philosophically repressed in the culture they founded." Indeed! Cavell could have as easily said that they are repressed in every other way also. Anyway, this negative but revealing beginning leads to the positive thought that at least Thoreau, in particular, has not separated philosophy from literature nor, more importantly, the reader from the writer. Now Cavell introduces the idea of the "fantastic": "Of all the writers who have suggested something like this idea, that the reader of the book, not the exceptional figures within it, is the fantastic, none can go beyond Thoreau's systematic notation of the idea, nor beyond his seriousness in claiming the uncanny vision [of the reader's through the writer's] as essential to philosophy—to the extent that philosophy is what attacks false necessities and false ideas of the necessary as in Rousseau, but no less in Plato and Descartes and Hume and Kant and Marx and Nietzsche and Heidegger and Wittgenstein."

"The inflection of the idea of the reader as fantastic is thus an idea of the reader's willingness to subject himself or herself to taking the eyes of the writer [and the writer of the reader's]. . . . Taking one another's eyes is the chance outside science to learn something new; which is to say outside science, to learn something. . . The fact of reading and writing, of the possibility of language as such, is the miracle, the fantastic."

We should now know that this ever-educating process is free and open to everyone. But given this, it still behooves us, with discernment and determination, to raise our sights and accept with pleasure the task of the text—a rewarding task that begins with those authors above, particularly, for us, Emerson and Thoreau. Only then, with these "texts of recovery," will we responsibly participate in what will prove to be the most self-liberating project of our lives.

Fantastic!

---

[1] Stanley Cavell, *In Quest for the Ordinary: Lines of Skepticism and Romanticism.* University of Chicago Press, 1988.

(*Art Source*, Winter 1991)

104

Book Review

Bourne Again
The Critical Renewal

Ah ne'er so dire a thrust of glory boast, Nor in the critic let the man be lost! Good nature and good sense must ever join, To err is human, to forgive divine.

"An Essay on Criticism," Alexander Pope

I am nothing if not critical. *Othello,* William Shakespeare

The Company of Critics; Social Criticism & Political Commitment in the Twentieth Century (1988) by Michael Walzer (professor of Social Science at the Institute for Advance Study, Princeton, NJ.) we observe that out of the twelve critics discussed, only two are Americans, only one native born.

Herbert Marcuse *(One Dimensional Man,* 1958), the better known, lived his last thirty years here to conclude a long academic career. Of Randolph Bourne (the native), who is relatively unknown today, Walzer says "that if one were to search for an American embodiment of the true intellectual, there is no more likely candidate than Randolph Bourne. Few Americans have set themselves so passionately to be intellectuals, and few have been so faithful to that calling. This description of Bourne is common in the critical literature. ..."

This statement must surely give one pause — why such obscurity? Is it that we as Americans are given only to that which has a certain utility? Or is it that there is a passing of fame, greatness and glory of all critical studies no matter how wide the original acceptance? (Allan Bloom's *The Closing of the American Mind,* 1988, a *New York Times* best seller with sales over one million, is a good example of this slide into near oblivion.)

However one answers the above questions, it will

become apparent that there is a need for good criticism, that there are critical performances that become forms of art and live forever.

For the most skeptical, there is the foremost realm of world literature, for here is found the highest and most noble examples of lasting criticism: In the Prophet's warnings; in Jesus's sermons; in Socrates's dialogues; in Augustine's confessions; in Chaucer's tales; in Cervante's dreams; in Shakespeare's soliloquies and sonnets; in Nietzche's ravings; in Emerson's essays; in Thoreau's witticisms; in Whitman's poetry. Pure criticism!

From the same realm, the voice of criticism, in a more imaginary sense, also resides: In Tolstoy's peasants; in Dostoevsky's madmen; in Dickens's waifs; in O'Neil's drunks; in Williams's degenerates; in Eliot's saints (and cats); in Becket's tramps and clowns; in Vonnegut's zainies. Critics all!

If in great literature one finds the closing defense for good criticism, this must not seem a rarefied or impossible task suitable only for "the lunatic, the lover, and the poet" and only taken up after a long process of elimination (of less fulfilling pursuits) at the end of one's life. In our beginning is our end and the guiding text for placing literature at the center of an early education is *The Child as Critic*, 1984, by Glenna Davis Sloan (introduced and inspired by the great Canadian literary critic, Northrop Fry). An "Education President" will do well by this guide when entering that vast wasteland called public education.

In criticism, through literature and around literature, resides the great eternal return. Randolph Bourne is not an anomaly and we are not still-born. There is a true second birth, a renewal that brings one, in due time, critically thus importantly full circle.

(Art Source, January 1992)

Review

Tutelage Two Thousand[1]

The Continued Necessity and Sufficiency of Self-Culture

"Soap and education are not as sudden as a massacre but they're more deadly in the long run!"

Mark Twain

My father, to impress importance, would often ask me: "Where is your tutelage? What is your tutelage? Do you have tutelage?" Tutelage derives from the Latin *tutela* meaning protection guardianship, instruction. Tutor and tutorial seen in the roles of teaching and instructing, especially privately are the more popular usages. For me, tutelage has evolved (as my father hoped it would) to mean the life long project of one's education.

My father's education, following his brother[2], began in the home, proceeded with hard work through and around high school, then through and around Yale University. In his time, few students from public high schools were admitted to private universities like Yale — little through and around. My father's questions began a working and passing of tutelage.

The Yale instructor about whom my father mostly spoke was the Robert Browning scholar, William Lyon Phelps. The heritage, the legacy, the tutelage of William Lyon Phelps is his introducing into the curriculum of colleges and universities (Yale first then all America) British and American contemporary literature—a heresy at the time (1900) and now due to multicultural interest—a heresy again!

William Lyon Phelps knew personally: Mark Twain, George Santayana, Thomas Hardy, William Butler Yeats, Stephen Vincent Benet, Sinclair Lewis, George Bernard Shaw, John Burroughs, A, E. Robinson, Ellen Glasgow, Robert Frost, T. S. Eliot, William Deans Howells, Henry James, J. M. Barrie, Vachel Lindsay, Edith Wharton, Joseph Conrad, Edna Ferber. I have photographs of Phelps with Thornton Wilder, G, K. Chesterton, John Galsworthy, and Henry Ford (Phelps spent his summers in the Thumb of Michigan).[3]

In his classic *New England: Indian Summer, 1865-1915,* Van Wyck Brooks announces: "With William Lyon Phelps, Yale had out-grown its earlier indifference to letters." In the earlier and equally classic *The Flowering of New England, 1815-1865,* he made the same announcement with Emerson's arrival at Harvard.

The old liberal, Arthur Schlesinger, Jr., in his most con-servative book to date, *Disuniting America* (1991), while lamenting the ill effects of multiculturalism, implicitly ac-knowledges that William Lyon Phelps established the canon for contemporary literature in his time.

Was this to be the tutelage under which I was to labor?

"Where is *the Life we have lost in living? Where is the Wisdom we have lost in knowledge? Where is the Knowkdge we have lost in information ?*"

T. S. Eliot, *The Rock*

Today, television presents a movie by Oliver Stone called "Wild Palms" which is also the title of a little known novel by William Faulkner, an author concerned with "the old verities and truths of the heart." The movie plots out a bleak and oppressive future (2007) where the Fathers (a religious cult— New Realism) battle the Friends (of freedom—an old and diminishing value). This takes place in a world (Los Angeles) that is a tyranny of techno-gadgets like virtual reality and free standing holograms—hardly a moving picture of the old verities and truths of the heart.

Today, I read in *The New York Times Magazine Supplement:* "The Telephone Transformed—Into Almost Everything"[1] by James Gleick, May 16,1993, about the coming technology in phone communication that makes current access look like the Dark Age and that "super-highways" of information are being financed by the current administration in Washington.

Today, I also read in *The New Times Book Review, Aug.* 29, 1993, about "Hyperfiction: Novels for the Computer," by Robert Coover. This is a new narrative art form that will be most familiar to children who use hypertext technology in their computer games. The advantage to "bounce around freely" choosing one's own direction through the novel is one of the alluring features offered to the computer reader. "Hyper" is an appropriate prefix for this process that makes a game of novels, permissiveness of freedom, and myopia of good eyes (and good minds).

One could celebrate the efficiency, ease and entertainment value of tools for the conveyance of print culture; one, however, must deplore the emerging end product, wisdom reduced to information served up electronically, even as it reigns supreme, for being, for the most part, trivial or meaningless.

The superiority of print culture over electronic culture is revealed, in part, in electronic culture's arrogant claim: The quality and quantity of time. This is a false claim due mainly to the fact that electronic culture is by nature passive. Print culture is by nature active which axiomatically assures the quality of time. Its independence from technology ironically assures the quantity of time. If one should question the active nature of print culture, one need only look into two sources (there are many): Stanley Fish, *Is There a Text in This Class?* and Stanley Cavel, *The Quest for Ordinary Language.*

As for cults, the only one on which to keep an eye is the cult of information. Super-highways of information will not lead to an educated electorate (pun?) but to a robotic, one dimensional mentality more given to "information sick-ness" than to enlightenment—producing a nation of numb-nots.

Is this to be the tutelage under which we must all die?

"There are no adventures like intellectual ones."

Henry James

Our tutelage needs only to be introduced. It waits surrounding us in people and the pages unto which they pass. Hours in the classroom are necessary but when a teacher ignites a student in a tutorial way, only then does an accident/miracle happen. (But, is this not, in part (with partner), self-initiation?) Only this is sufficient. An example: The Shakespearean actor/director Kenneth Branagh in an interview with Charlie Rose (PBS) spoke of spending hours in a Shakespeare course with lectures and student readings but nothing happened (to him). In another Shakespeare course (both required), under another teacher, one insight did it (never mind that it was the role of lust in *Romeo and Juliet).* Branagh who came from a non-literary background was on his way to self-fulfillment. In the classroom too, when anything important happens, it is always a matter of self-education.

Father, mother, sister, brother, teacher, friend and the only worthy repository of their repeated efforts, the book in its classic, sacred and sage form, reminding, redeeming the reader begins and continues this ever-educating process.

This is the only tutelage that is self-renewing, self-supporting; when necessary, it disciplines, when sufficient, it frees.

---

[1] Although this essay or review bears the same opening title as the 2000 installment V of "The Declaration of America" series at the beginning of this book, in this earlier (1993) article the author was reviewing the general drift of contemporary books and articles written previously that bear on the subject of education and "self-culture".

[2]Adrian (Tony) Morse later became a provost at Pennsylvania State University for 27 years (The Morse Era) and after helped establish (at the request of President Eisenhower) the University of New Delhi (India).

[3] *William Lyon Phelps: Autobiography with Letters,* Oxford University Press, 1939. t Otsego County Library, including 3 other volumes of Brooks' that begin and conclude one of the best literary histories of our country.

(*Art Source*, Winter 1993)

Foreword

Views from a Hermitage[1]

In the woods of northern Michigan, there is a group of friends who get together occasionally during warm summer evenings for stimulating discussions. I will call it "The Gaylord Group": A professor of mathematics at the City University New York, a former editor of *The Philadelphia Bulletin* newspaper, a philosopher and former head of the philosophy department at Vanderbilt University, Nashville, a writer out of the University of Michigan, Ann Arbor, and a Catholic theologian, with doctorates from the University of Ottawa and Université St-Paul, Ottawa.

Richard Kropf is the theologian whose essays are presented in this book and I am the one, as a writer, who was asked to select out of nearly two-hundred such essays, to glean the important, pertinent, and most interesting ones for public perusal. Kropf's essays, which appear under the title of "Religion in Today's World" have been published periodically in the local *Gaylord Herald Times*. His voice and views were most impressive at our discussions.

The most insightful comment about Kropf offered to me was made by the philosopher of the group, John Compton, son of Arthur Compton, a Nobel prize winner in physics and a member of the Manhattan Project. He stated that Kropf, the only member of the group who continues to live year round in the solitude of the northwoods, "leads the most authentic and envied life of a real philosopher."

As a skeptical and secular thinker, my criterion for selection needs an explanation. Composed with the goal of exploring the influence of religious thought, for better or for worse, on many aspects of contemporary life in this world, I had to choose carefully what made one essay, written within the context, if not strict Catholic doctrine, then a Christianity more general, more acceptable over another. Kropf's strength, which I feel lies in this selection and is most represented in all his writings, is humanistic, ecumenical, liberal, and rational. While his vocation may have taken the direction that it has due to the example and advice of the American monk and spiritual writer, Thomas Merton, nevertheless, the cosmic and evolutionary perspectives of his thought reflect the strong influence of his intellectual hero, the controversial French priest-paleontologist-philosopher, Pierre Teilhard de Chardin. In this, Kropf's thought is truly "Catholic", embracing a wide spectrum of views and reflecting not the monolithic entity that the Church is thought to be by many, but, like most of Christendom, diverse and universal as also all good thinking can and must be.

Kropf's essays address real problems that any concerned person must confront if he or she is to honestly have a conscious and intelligent life. This is very simple on the surface, but simplicity of this sort opens doors that esoteric doctrine and convoluted thought won't and can't, even for the devout. Kropf cuts across all pious rhetoric, jargon, evasiveness, and incurious certainty.

I am experienced in these matters by my own secular approach, first as a student of intellectual history, the study of which I still pursue, to one of the oldest literary efforts: the Bible (preferably The King James Version — William Shakespeare, as the joke goes, being on the translating committee). The Bible is one of the most inspiring sources for capturing the drama and dilemmas of life. Its influence on Western literature is inestimable. Great literature led by the Bible rises above science and its twin, systematic philosophy, both the most honorable of human pursuits, to lead us through the light of life, the dark of death.

Richard Kropf has shown me time again this life supporting awareness making his essays, even those couched in learned orthodoxy or unorthodoxy, a joyful personal yet universal fund of truth bearing insights and inspired revelations.

Anthony Jenckes Morse
Gaylord, Michigan
June, 2007

---

[1] *Views from a Hermitage: Reflections on Religion in Today's World* by Richard W. Kropf. Latham, MD: Rowman & Littlefield Publishers, 2008. Republished (2nd, expanded edition) by Stellamar Publications, 2015.

114

Einstein and the Image of God

As a foreword or preface to this book[1], the author Richard Kropf, who has been one of my closest friends over the past thirty or so years, asked me to compose a survey of readings leading up and through "The New Atheism" movement that is one of the subjects of this new book. In fact, I had loaned him most of these books — or even bought a few extra copies just for him to read and have handy for reference, since he lives in a rather isolated area in the woods of Northern Michigan.

But first let me make explicit my own position. As I have stated and written in the past about God, in the face of this "mysterious unknown, agnosticism is the proper stance. With an acclaimed revelation though one must study and seek the best explanation, and short of dogmatism - judge! Agnosticism in this case leads to relativism, little dialogue, and less thinking." Or again, as Nietzsche said: "To judge is the nut of existence." It answers the biblical "Judge not, that ye be not judged." Thus, of late, I have, like Albert Einstein, adopted Spinoza's God.

For me, and Kropf acknowledges, my studies in history and philosophy ended with an Intellectual History undergraduate degree from the University of Michigan (1955-59). There, I was to take, most influentially, two semesters of "Existentialism" from Walter Kaufmann, visiting professor of philosophy from Princeton University. Kaufmann is internationally recognized for his translations (Basic Books and Every Man Series) of the philosopher Friedrich Nietzsche and largely responsible for having introduced him to mid-

[1] Richard W. Kropf, *Einstein and the Image of God: A Response to Contemporary Atheism.* Stellamar Publications, 2015.

twentieth century America. Kaufmann is also recognized for his reinterpretation of Nietzsche as a Pan-European visionary. This is against his once-assumed influence on, and corresponding blame for having provided the philosophical underpinnings for Nazism. And I would credit Kaufmann's, *Critique of Philosophy and Religion"* as having set up my contextualized reading program agenda for most of my life.

Accordingly, I spent the 1960's and '70's being guided by philosopher-scholar Theodore Roszak who is best known for his 1969 book, *The Making of the Counterculture.* This in turn involved reading mostly secular poets and thinkers from usually Lotusland — California. Then it was on to the next period with the "Colossal Critic", Harold Bloom of Yale and philosopher Stanley Calvell of Harvard. Both reintroduced me to Emerson, Thoreau, and Whitman, but this time with the distinction of emphasizing in these founding thinkers their Deistic inclinations.

But the thinker who most prefaces "The New Atheism" is the "Prince of Pragmatism", philosopher Richard Rorty. Rorty's earliest (1979) book *Philosophy and The Mirror of Nature,* remains a major watershed in modern philosophy. He particularly castigates Plato for his other worldly views — Rorty's mirror being Plato's wall in the cave being itself the Grand Illusion! "Correspondence" for Rorty is a theistic ruse. Rorty was the main target of attack of the very conservative Lutheran-turned-Catholic, Fr. Richard John Neuhaus, in his 2009 counter-cultural protest book, *American Babylon.*

Now, on to "The New Atheism" and the "New Atheists" of this current movement:

Christopher Hitchens was an Oxford-educated English journalist and critic whose books I had read before hearing him on stage at the Apollo Theater in London, 2002. This was a full five years before his 2007 international best seller *God is not Great: How Religion Poisons Everything*. The phrase "New Atheism" had not been coined but Hitchens was a very colorful and controversial character, even then. I was not familiar with his anti - religious stance so I was surprised to hear him say "The axis of evil is Judaism, Christianity, and Islam"! In a short chat with Hitchens in the Apollo Lounge after, I asked him if I had heard correctly. "Yes" he answered. We talked about some of his books — one of which I had just read, *Letters to a Young Contrarian*" (2001). He said that this book was better than the one being promoted that evening! I was getting the tone of his polemic and a first-hand preview of "The New Atheism".

Subsequently, Sam Harris's best seller, *The End of Faith*, won the 2005 PEN Award for Nonfiction and is published in more than fifteen languages. He has a degree in philosophy from Stanford University and a PhD in neuroscience from UCLA, and to all appearances at the time, seemed to be an unwavering materialist, and hence, atheist. So I was surprised to read in his new 2014 book, *Waking Up: A Guide to Spirituality Without Religion*, about how much time Harris has spent on meditation and Buddhism. His scientific approach produces a most convincing picture. Harris says that religion is especially rife with bad ideas, calling it "one of the most perverse misuses of intelligence we have devised".

Richard Dawkins is an evolutionary biologist and English ethologist at Cambridge. His 2006 book *The God Delusion*", capitalizing on his popular and controversial *The Selfish Gene* (1976) started to solidify the "New Atheist" movement with the three already mentioned. These "Four Horsemen" of the movement would meet often. In this book Dawkins contends that a supernatural creator almost certainly does not exist and that religious faith is a delusion - "a fixed false belief".

Daniel Dennett is the only professional philosopher of the group, with a "DPhil" from Oxford University and a teaching post at Tufts University. While Kropf and I have shared our impressions of Dennett's 1995 *Darwin's Dangerous Idea*, and his 2006 *Breaking The Spell: Religion as a Natural Phenomenon*, Kropf remains convinced that while Dennett is a good philosopher of science that Dennett's grasp of or utter contempt for ontology (the science or philosophy of being), is all too obvious.

The above four formed the original group, dubbing themselves "The Four Horsemen of the New Atheism". However, as Kropf notes, there had been, all along until his death in 2014, a fifth aspirant to that exclusive group, one whose atheistic credentials had long predated the other four. This was Victor J. Stenger, a long-time professor of physics at the University of Hawaii, capped with an emeritus post as Professor of Philosophy at the University of Colorado. His dozen or so books, the first dating back to the late 1980s, and most of them dealing with the universe and its origins, are all more or less explicitly atheistic in outlook, culminating with his 2012 *God and The Folly of Faith: The Incompatibility of Science and Religion.* In it he continued to be a strong advocate for removing the influence of religion from scientific research, commercial activity, and the political process, and he coined the popular phrase "Science flies you to the moon. Religion flies you into buildings." Kropf also noted that Stenger, unlike "the four horsemen", seems to have understood not only the full breadth of the scientific, and especially cosmological, and ultimately ontological issues — as well as (having been raised a Catholic) having some respect for the theologians who wrestled with these issues in past ages and continue to do so.

Last on this list of books of note which seem to be dedicated to aggressively promoting atheism, we have Lawrence Krauss' 2012 best-selling *A Universe from Nothing: Why There is Something Rather than Nothing*. Krauss specializes as a professor of theoretical physics and cosmology at MIT. Krauss states that the premise that something cannot come nothing is often used as an argument for the existence of an uncaused cause, or creator. But in a dazzling display of double-talk he affirms that the laws of physics allow for the universe to be created from nothing, because, as he finally admits (in Chapter 9), "Nothing Is Something".

Thus ends the brief survey of atheistic books that Kropf and I have studied and discussed over the last ten or so years. There are many more books on atheism, some good, some bad. For a fuller survey of the subject, one should consult Peter Watson's 2014 *The age of Atheism: How We Have Sought to Live Since the Death of God*.

However, there are two more writers I would like to mention, if I may, to which I have given recently much attention. I have read all of Lewis Lapham's books (written while he was editor of *Harper's Magazine*) and from its beginning, seven years ago, I have subscribed to *Lapham's Quarterly*, a journal most brilliant and beautiful. Each issue on one subject only has a mixture of authors ancient to modern, world wide, with attending art work. Each issue is a testimony to the monumental multiplicity of minds on our planet. Lewis Lapham is the master of juxtaposition and a strong proponent of secularism.

Another writer who represents the pinnacle (for now) of all my readings related to my own quest for "The Declaration of America" is Matthew Stewart and his *Nature's God: The Heretical Origins of the American Republic"*, (2014).

Stewart is a historian and philosopher who in this latest book traces from Epicurus through Spinoza how revolutionary the American Revolution was and is. This revolution is set in stone: on Thomas Jefferson's tomb and under glass - The Declaration of Independence and our Constitution. Unlike "The New Atheists", Stewart, like Albert Einstein did, does not deny peoples need for religion, but Stewart believes in a religion of freedom.

So where does all this leave "The "New Atheism" and "The New Atheist" and how is Kropf going to deal with them? First, I think we must go back to the philosopher Walter Kaufmann. His 1950 *Nietzsche: Philosopher, Psychologist, and Anti-Christ* made Kaufmann famous, for he more than anyone else made intellectuals shed their misconceptions about Nietzsche and recognized him as one of at the most important thinkers in Western philosophy and one of the greatest writers in German literature. But this was not the case in 1947 when Kaufmann arrived at Princeton University. He was introduced to Albert Einstein — who questioned him about the thesis on which he was working. Upon hearing Kaufmann, the shocked Einstein responded: "But that is simply dreadful!" So it seems that Kaufmann had his work cut out for himself.

The other misconception about Nietzsche was the failure of the public knowing the total context of Nietzsche's claim that "God is dead". "God is dead. God remains dead...And we have killed him. How shall we comfort ourselves, the murderers of all murderers?" ("The Gay Science" sec: 125, translated by Walter Kaufmann, *The Portable Nietzsche*). In this same vein of blame, Kaufmann coined the word "empiricide" and so science and rationality of man are responsible for God's death! Ten years after my graduation I attended a lecture by Kaufmann at the

University of Michigan and talked to him briefly afterwards. He died all too soon ten years later, in 1980, at the age of 59.

When it comes to thinking about other religions other than the one in which we were raised, we are all atheists! And is it really God we are talking about? When you read the "New Atheists" you see that they are, really not so much reacting to arguments in favor of there being a God, but rather more to various and different aspects of the human predicament: war, poverty, disease, suffering, nature, the cosmos etc. Can we really know for certain the beginning (cause), the purpose (plan), the end (eternity) of life? Christopher Hitchens preferred to be called anti-theist than an atheist — as does Lawrence Krauss. And in their angry outbursts are mostly talking about certain people and events and the ideas that produced them or were produced by them, but not God. Sam Harris being a neuroscientist speaks of the mind that is physically only the brain, part of our body. Thus, to Harris there is no soul and therefore (however illogically argued from that) no God either. Richard Dawkins advocates evolutionary processes, all physical, all observable and with no evidence of God. Daniel Dennett and Victor J. Stenger talk of suns with beginnings and ends, and of planets with beginnings and ends — but no God.

And so we end all the above with the materialistic position of not so much of atheism but agnosticism. Conversely the Abrahamic religions (Judaism, Christianity, Islam} rely for their foundations on the various revealed "truths" that have come to them through holy persons, divinely caused events, sacred scripture. In his new book Kropf will wend his way through these various revelations to counter particularly the more negative agnosticism and atheisms currently afoot. Therefore I will end this preface by taking a look at two thinkers Kropf feels supply some answers to this important discus-sion: Philosopher Baruch Spinoza and scientist Albert Einstein.

Let us hear from Spinoza first:

> Nature does not work with an end in view. For the eternal and infinite Being which we call God or Nature, acts by the same necessity as that whereby it exists...Therefore, as he does not exist for the sake of an end, so neither does he act for the sake of an end; of his existence and his action there is neither origin nor end.

This is monism, materialism, pantheism, naturalism, determinism, and theism, and for some atheism.

There is today a reviving interest in Spinoza. British historian Jonathan Israel is one of the world's leading historians of the Enlightenment. His *"Radical Enlightenment and the Making of Modernity 1650-1750"* (2001) emphasizes the role of 17th century Holland and particularly Spinoza on most European thinkers of the time {and later}. Another interesting book suggested by a mutual friend of Kropf's and mine is *Looking for Spinoza: Joy, Sorrow, and the Feeling Brain* (2003), by Antonio Damasio, head of the neurology department of the University of Iowa. His book is mainly a study of the workings of the mind, its problems with solutions primarily suggested by the insights of Spinoza. The last chapter titled "Who's There?" leaves us with this conclusion: "If you ask of Spinoza's perspective, Hamlet's disquieting, inaugural question, "Who's there?—meaning who is out there to let us persist as our endeavor of self-preservation mandates—the answer is unequivocal. No one. Aloneness is the stark reality, of Christ on the cross and Spinoza in the crushed pillows of his deathbed. And yet,

Spinoza conjures up a means to elude that reality, a noble illusion meant to let us face the music and dance."

Einstein said that he believed in Spinoza's God. This religious feeling "of the profounder sort of scientific minds...takes the form of a rapturous amazement at the harmony of natural law, which reveals an intelligence of such superiority that, compared with it, all the systematic thinking and acting of human beings is an utterly insignificant reflection...Hence it is precisely among the heretics of every age that we find men who were filled with the highest kind of religious feeling and were in many cases regarded by their contemporaries as atheist, sometimes also saints. Looked at in this light, men like Democritus, Francis of Assisi, and Spinoza are closely akin to one another" (Einstein, *The World As I See It*. 1934).

This is as far as this preface can go in examining the directions that Kropf takes us. He continues, most importantly, with the French Jesuit and paleontologist Pierre Teilhard de Chardin, concerning whom he is one of the leading experts living. In the ending of his book, Kropf creates a synthesis that is not a collection of dogmas, doctrines, or creeds, but a sublime thinking that rises above the various certainties usually offered and this thinking celebrates the greatness and goodness of our mysterious and marvelous created being. At the end, you have a philosopher and a theologian who expertly guides us between the stubborn rocks of religious conviction and the shifting shoals of science.

Anthony Jenckes Morse, April, 2015

Part IV

Verse

"It is art that makes life,
Makes interest,
Makes importance."
(Henry James)

Human-Nature

While searching for the Mysterious
Morel, I mutter to myself: "I must
find these God-Blasted Beauties
before the deer do."

So, like a one-eyed Cyclops, I big-
Foot my way over the forest floor,
acting the lordly surveyor of this
strange and marvelous universe.

But, I do not participate!

Therefore, when I transfix in the
Cross-hairs of my barbarous brain
Shroomus Erectus I swoop down
with vengeance and glee and short
of root and all take it for my little
own.

Tony Morse

Conquering Heroes

"Freedom and life are earned by those alone
Who conquer them each day anew." Goethe, *Faust*

ZZZZZzzz There it is again!
Something is in a deep, heavy sleep. O dear,
breathing in long, hibernating intervals, digesting
winter. **ZZZZZzzz**

I stop breathing and listen. There it is again - a loud
to quiet **ZZZZZzzz.** But who, what, where?

There she is — reading but her exhaling breath does
not match. Nor does mine though all I hear now is
my pounding heart. **ZZZZZzzz**

We began— just the two of us in this woodsy cabin.
How did it get into the crawl space below the floor?
ZZZZZzzz

I won't say anything — she'll only scream and cry and
I won't be able to hear. **ZZZZZzzz**

I move to the wood stove for warmth. A drop of
water from a pan lid drops sizzling onto the hot
stove top – **ZZZZZzzz**

Through the window I stare at the winter wonder.
Oh, you fearless reality-seeker, you have made it
through another day.
What new mystery will unnerve you tomorrow, cast
adrift a quaking doubt upon your sleepless soul?
ZZZZZzzz
                                                            Tony Morse

Of Course:

I will go where the wild ones go, To the shade & shine of
streams, to golden shores, To lands open that put the
sun in your belly, To places of spirit that feed blood and
bone.
 But don't ask me when— you will know.

I will sing wild words wild men sing. In tomes more
brave than heroic deeds, In sacred sources hard &
strange & sure, In fearless out door minds, minds of
winter, minds of night.
 But don't ask me where — you will know.

I will sleep where the wild gods sleep
Where Greek dramatist & Roman orators & Persian
poets sleep, Where heroes & saints of myth & legend are
warmed by the fires of oblivion, Where one dreams
eternal to hear the heretic's holy hymn.
 But don't ask me why—you will know.

Tony Morse

Shaking Down to Zero

Humourously titled so, it hung in one of those post 1960's galleries so prevalent on the West Coast.

A long, vertical painting of a dancing, laughing, rattling skeleton —a painting some would find crude, irreverant, adolescently revolutionary.

But it did strike up the classic theme —Danse Macabre — the dance of death.

From the shake, rattle and roll of white boney fingers in full circle fell: Dice; cards; cocktail glasses; a full female figure, upside down and askew (so unflattering and yes ladies, it does take two to dance), in a black evening dress with loosened high heel shoes (definitely not the severe woman of my dreams); a sleek, finned-out, all chromed automobile; a colonial styled (a starter) suburban home with boat, camper, and recreational vehicle not far behind.

Through all this rained green printed paper— money matter that makes all this happen.

Missing was one large screen to represent that insatiable visual diet to which we are turned and tuned. Missing also are those more mental but still material habits - sports, travel, hobbies and careers ("Does a deer have a career?" was once asked of me).

For me, it has been a mixed blessing—this travail through a litany of loved objects.

However, this I know: There is zero and there is Nothing; there is death and there is Death.

Sadly, shamefully, (but really fearfully) the lesson above is usually learned too late: We grow old, we grow up; one can be properly prepared to receive the Great Song in breast and brain through lit and lilt, finally arriving at that crucially important point of actually being able to live.

Tony Morse

Take Dover Road

You're lost!
Take Dover Road to Dover Pond.
Fly over the Sparr Valley.
Swim down the Pigeon River.
Walk through the meadow of poplar and pine.
Now you're found.
Take Dover Road to Dover Pond.

Tony Morse

Who?

Who is singing The Great Song
now that the Great Grey Poet is gone?
Now that The Beatific One howling over his courage-teacher
is retired?

Only soul-sucked slaves surround me –
with purchase orders & briefs & abstracts in hand –
And I hear not a Holy Writ.

Who is dancing the Great Dance
now that The Gentleman Dancing in the Dark is gone?
Now that children with bells & flowers tethered to their toes
have retired?

Only rich runners surround me –
rushing for the ticket, on the take –
And I see not a graceful step.

Who is musing the Great Music
now that He Who Hears Within is gone?
Now that song-poets blasted by tweeting wolves
have retired?

Only dissonant noise surrounds me –
we have all become the Grateful Deaf –
And I move not to a rhythm of soft sounds.

Who is sculpting the Great Sculpture
now that the Ugly Angel who would not finish the slave is
gone?
Now that togas & gowns & ropes of silk
hang retired?

Only wire ties surround me –
stick men of metal made (in Japan) with briefcases & business
cards that boast: DONT TOUCH!
And I feel not the cool clay of a white robe.

Who is painting the Great Portrait
now that Soul-full Eyes of Many Costumes is gone?
Now that those of flesh & form & flow lacking light
have retired?

Only hard & dark images surround me –
sharply edging us out of this world –
And I imagine not a person's face deeply lit with long lived
lines.

Tony Morse[1]

---

[1] The author's answers: Whitman, Astaire, Beethoven, Michelangelo, Rembrandt

Word Under Glass

The word under glass is not
a monument nor moment entombed
but life temporarily off the street
to celebrate in museum fashion —
in the Foelger, Huntington, Morgan, Hammer —
its perennial and primal importance.

People pass onto pages
if they pass onto anyplace
and so the word under glass
is eternal and shines of its own light —
unlike those flat, glaring images that direct the eye only
and the more you see the less you get.

Film fails to fulfill;
it does not resonate, adhere, or consume;
it is, as we are told, to look through a glass darkly
or into a hazy (filmy!) mirror thus remaining children.

Film can't do metaphor (nor irony nor ambiguity)
as the word can, only simile
and simile is a secondary condition of metaphor:
Film is like; the word is.

Film's only glory is silence (Chaplin, photography)
for it is inarticulate, incapable of thought, dumb
(sound is only voice-over—redundant and distracting).
The viewer becomes passive unlike the reader for while
one sees creation, one does not hear
(know and react with) the creator.

134

The word under glass is imagination perfect
and when in our hands again it never fails to perfect
because face to face
it tells the most beautiful tale
and tells the most immortal truth.

Tony Morse

Mythic Me

While we still have words, let us pen
A painful sonnet of humble thoughts and deeds
Known once to heroes and saints to never mend
The illusions that cloud our nearest needs.

We wear many hats (and wonder not the sun).
We becomes life's mask and so are hidden —
With a tuck here, a dab there — all in one —
No one to all and to ourselves forbidden.

Behind masks, moods challenge role upon role —
Fake fortresses of ditches and delusions —
Deceptions that stop us from becoming whole.
We are hanged between hope and confusions.

These lines do battle long for you to see.
I'll write many more to see the mythic me.

Tony Morse

Empty Pockets

It is a vision now.

Then, he walked with beard and belted robe
with no pockets.
Now, we all have pockets sown into our genes.
Then, for summer things: stones, a knife, string, a frog or two.
Now, for winter things.
But I, wizened, arrive like his third daughter, a love
wanting nothing or like his only son, naked.
Me, with empty pockets.

It is a vision now.

Tony Morse

NOW

A morning star lights the beginning of our daily round.
We work west down brown paths following the sun's blaze.
We walk in an antique land around old grey stumps
    and through a growing forest that promises a sky of green.
Yet we ask for more space, for more time.
And though we are at the center, in the heart of all,
    we search a past long ago, a future far away.
We wonder where and wonder when.

In the high noon sun the mystery we seek
    [it is the person we meet]
        is exposed to doubts and dissected easily —
           and who is to know? Is it not so?
This is our travail, this traveling down a long lit afternoon
      with eyes down, grounded 'till sundown.
    [Did we see it go behind those plush hills
      of this water-radiant plateau?]
Evening shadows bring us to a table set —
    by a lake, on a river, in a darkening green.
Now is served a commemorative repast that gives respite.
In moonlight, with hands held, we hear a chorus
    of loving persons present answer with the night
      [and a new star.]

        It is not there, then. No
        It is here, now. So

Tony Morse

APPENDIX:
ON SEARCHING FOR TRUTH

FROM TRUTH TO APPROXIMATION
By Raymond Macdonald

In 2005, philosophers Richard Rorty and Pascal Engel engaged in a debate variously entitled "What's the the Use of Truth?" Or in French: *"A Quoi Bon la Verite?"* (What is the good of truth?). One title might be called metaphysical, the other pragmatic. But this categorization of titles seems not to have been notice by the editors of the volume.

In any case, in the debate, Engel defended the traditional use of the term truth, while Rorty called for it's retirement, deeming it useless in solving any problem in the real world - consistent with the position taken in his now classic text, "Philosophy and the Mirror of Nature" (1979). This essay takes the position that Rorty's conclusion on the fatuity of the term truth is correct — but his reasons and recommendations are ill-conceived, for reasons which follow.

FIRST: GEOMETRY IS NOT THE LANGUAGE OF NATURE
Galileo Galilei, the famous 16th century astronomer, stated that "The great book of nature is written in mathematical symbols." Four centuries later Albert Einstein, in his essay "A Mathematician's Mind," takes a more contrite modern view. According to Einstein, nature has no language. He states that insofar as a term or concept seeks to define reality, any geometrical term must be approximate and not certain:

Conventional words or other signs have to be sought for laboriously only in a secondary stage (of thought), when the mentioned associative play is sufficiently established and can be reproduced at will. (Albert Einstein, *Ideas and Opinions*, p. 36, from "A Mathematician's Mind")

Why are mathematical terms approximate in relation to reality? Einstein reasons it is from the independent nature of the human mind and its inventions.

Here we give a somewhat different reason involving the nature of reality. This is to say that nature is a constant process of change; mathematics, on the other hand, employs a constant vocabulary. How can a constant repetitive method, a human invention, capture a constantly changing non-human subject? How can constant representation deal with constant change? By approximation, is the only answer Einstein gives to this problem. This statement takes the problem out of a mathematical context and makes it into one of language generally. How can we deal with the language of communication applied to an ever changing reality? Einstein answers this as well:

The words or the language, as they are written or spoken, do not seem to play any role in my mechanism of thought. The psychical entities which seem to serve as elements in thought are certain signs and more or less clear images which can be "voluntarily" reproduced and combined. (Albert Einstein, *Ideas and Opinions*, p. 35, from "A Mathematician's Mind")

To the point: whether "mind and nature" or "semantics and nature", the conclusion is the same. In either view, we cannot expect conformity of one with the other. Not truth but approximation is the closest fit to be made. Rorty does not consider this yawning gap between mind or language and reality thus exposing the thesis to the confusion of a liberal arts semantic.

SECOND: CONTRARIES AND CONTRADICTIONS DO NOT APPLY TO NATURE

Aristotle states that processes that result in addition or subtraction are of two kinds: contradictions and contraries. The definitions of these terms by him are as follows:

> Contradiction is an opposition which has no medium in respect to itself (*Politics* A-1). Contraries cannot possibly be inherent in the same thing at one and the same time. (*De Interpretatione* 1-14)

Contradictions require no middle term. Thus the concepts of just or unjust, rational or irrational, true or false - these terms are either one or the opposite. Contraries on the other hand envision a possible infinity of middle terms. Contraries thus provide the option of gradual growth or decline: as in more or less, stronger or weaker, better or worse. The point is contradictions have nothing to do with reality. Contraries are closer to the continual changes and gradual movement of nature. The distinction of true or false cannot apply to nature. Thus Rorty says:

> A person is sincere when she says what she thinks she is justified in believing. This will, automatically, be what she believes to be true. (Richard Rorty, *What's the Use of Truth?* p.42)

The problem with this statement is that an average person does not think in terms of true or false. These are terms which do not have an ordinary significance. People think in terms of more or less - where all assertions of fact are tested to determine the extent to which they can be believed. This is a common mistake - the confusion between contraries and contradictions. It is something Rorty might have considered, to bring his discourse into closer harmony with pragmatic thought.

THIRD: WORDS ARE SYMBOLS

"A word is a symbol" according to the British philosopher Alfred North Whitehead, in his writing on language in *"Symbolism: Its Meaning and Effect"* (1929).

What does describe reality then, if not words? There is the supposition that reality is found in antiquated systems of law, legislation, and religion, but in fact it is not found in language at all. Language does not begin in the street as common language, assumed by philosophers. Rather we should begin with the earliest forms of speech still existent with people living among animals and tribally. We can look first to infants, in their efforts at communication; look to traffic control signs, that guide behavior; and to hand and body gestures, that use simple signs. With these forms we should build a new grammar, beginning with things that occur in the here and now.

As an eye-witness, this would be the limit of our testimony, and as an eye-witness much scientific speculation would be reduced to just that—approximate and speculative.

In other words, truth is not the obvious aim of most speech. And where it is, it is carefully conditioned and circumscribed to work in the here and now. Limits which were not specified, but instead the full spectrum was, included pell-mell, by Rorty.

> The same relations between thought, language, and reality obtain in every cultural domain. If one discourse has the

capacity to represent the world, then all discourses have that capacity. If one of them "fits" the world, then they all do so equally. (Richard Rorty, *"What's the Use of Truth?"* p. 36)

Rorty's theory of language is problematic because he does not seem to see that there is anything behind language, and therefore he does not consider the aesthetic dimension - this is what puts us in contact with reality. The aesthetic dimension as well as the epistemological dimension are pre-linguistic. As Einstein recounts, when working on a theory, he would move objects in space, in a non-verbal realm, before eventually translating them into words for the public. In eliminating the epistemological dimension, Rorty is eliminating Einstein's pre-linguistic realm and his theory of reality.

FOURTH: SYMBOLS REQUIRE CONSENT

As I was walking down the street with my German Shepherd some years ago, he suddenly froze, and for the moment, I did as well. Until I saw the object of his fixation — a half-sized statue of a groom. The dog moved cautiously until he could smell the object, at which time, finding no scent, he gave it up and went on to examine the lawn down the street. It occurred to me that either the object must be alive or it was of no interest to him whatsoever. My dog had no system of symbols, for symbols require consent, and he did not have the faculties to understand or consent to such a system.

There are not different words or vocabularies for different subject matters as Rorty contends, except by agreement. We can use any word for anything we wish, according to the French philosopher, Henri Bergson, according to his statement in *Introduction to Metaphysics* (1903) — providing that we use the same word for the same thing to the same person. This total liberation of language from objects in the world imposes only one requirement to be understood and that is consent and understanding of the hearer. Primitive use of the word truth must end—what is wanted is a rigorous analysis of language to supply its omission.

FIFTH: A PICTURE CANNOT BE SEEN THROUGH WORDS

No word of number of words can supply a "mirror of nature" as Rorty asserts. A Chinese proverb says a picture is worth a thousand words. But this proportion could be expanded to an infinity of words. No number of words can supply a picture to a blind person. The mirror of nature is created, only if he or she can see the pictures. "A mirror of nature" what does this mean?

The sole and exclusive power of creation lies with the senses invoked, be it sight, hearing, taste, touch, or smell. All invocations of a sensory experience must address the sense involved. Words can not be or serve as a so-called mirror. Words only work as symbols to jar the memory of the hearer to reference the visual memory of or the sense — to replicate the sense invoked.

Thus Rorty would speak of different vocabularies to handle different subject matters in a kind of University of Chicago pluralism. The problem with this method of proceeding is that everything depends on the arbitrary selection of a particular vocabulary from which it follows that everything is as arbitrary as the selection itself.

In contrast, by beginning with the immediate at hand, in such a state that we could testify first-hand to what we see, hear, touch, taste, or smell, no arbitrary selection of a total vocabulary is involved. All that is involved is a symbolic reference to such a sensory experience. Thus the denomination of such things outside the immediate reference are hypothetical or conjectural. But this is what the scientific academia should admit — that all of its universal portraits of the cosmos are based on hypothesis and conjectures — some tightly schematized, others less so.

To hear a leading science writer of *The New York Times* explaining the confirmation of Einstein's theory of the existence of gravitational waves many light-years away, as a search for scientific "truth" ("Gravitational Waves Detected, Confirming Einstein's Theory", *The New York Times*, Feb. 11, 2016) — causes one to wonder whether Einstein and Whitehead have spent time illuminating the theoretical nature of these matters in vain.

IN CONCLUSION

Fixed science came to an end with Einstein's implied refutation of Galileo assertion that geometry is the language of nature. He corrects Galileo to assert that when mathematics is applied to reality, it must be an approximation. The reason for this revision is that nature is constantly changing, whereas mathematics employs a fixed vocabulary of symbols. Whitehead's analysis of symbols is more radical than Einstein's, in that he shows that all words are symbols, with the result that no statement can give more than a partial indication of the present situation, or of things to come. Bergson, on his part, argues that one can use any word one wants describe anything, but one must be consistent if they wish to be understood.

But these proposals are rejected by Rorty's high-end pluralistic analysis, which compares philosophical methods, and ends by disallowing everything certain. He might have considered different degrees of probability and usefulness for

146

various ventures, which is illustrated by the reconsidered semantic primitivism offered in this essay — such as: What are an infant's first words and what to they refer to? — is found in infant speech, animal sounds and traffic signals. How are traffic signs erected, showing "stop", "curve" and "intersection"? What is the one word that animal trainers use in instructing animals to "sit", "stay", "come", and other such expressions? This is where grammar should start.

Building on these references, communication should begin with simple gestures, as illustrated, in the here and now, not hypothetical philosophical generalizations — the form of Rorty's approach. Beginning with abstract theories, with each contending for legitimacy, he ends unable to find one position superior to any other.

The here and now — what we can see, hear, taste, touch, and smell — warrants its inclusion and acceptance into any systematic inquiry. Failing to include these forms of primitive analysis leaves the argument open to contention — and the inconclusiveness of Rorty's argument.

Raymond Macdonald
April 2016

AGREEMENTS / DISAGREEMENTS
By Anthony Jenckes Morse

It is the summer of 2016. Except for a few trips: Egypt, Italy, France, New England and Florida the last nine years have been spent reading and communing.

The communing part takes place at Starbucks [its mermaid logo a reminder] in the village of Grosse Pointe City. At least four afternoons a week there is a group of men and women who gather to read and talk. The subjects for discussion range from philosophy, politics, religion, books and movies.

For the purpose of most of the subjects in this book, the above appendix by Ray Macdonald was solicited from a person who I thought had the finest mind of the group. Ray attended several colleges including law school and the University of Chicago, where he edited a course by Richard McKeon. McKeon was the Dean of the Division of the Humanities at Chicago and is important for editing with an introduction, the Random House, "The Basic Works of Aristotle", 1941, which is still available. I have an original boxed edition.

Ray subsequently taught rhetoric ["Rhetoric", an important essay by Aristotle] at the University of California, Berkley. He left academia to continue the practice of law until quite recently. I think his knowledge of law influences constructively his method of philosophical thinking. He doesn't agree with me on this matter.

The above Appendix by Ray Macdonald is the result of many hours of discussion between the two of us. We both owned and read, "What's the Use of Truth", by Richard Rorty and Pascal Engel, (Columbia University Press, New York], before we met. I also wrote Part V of my "Declaration of America", 1999, relying in part on Rorty. Ray and I do agree on Rorty's importance in American philosophy. Ray only goes further with the investigation: "Rorty's conclusion on the futility of the term truth is correct – but his reason and recommendations are ill-conceived." There is no disagreement with Ray's conclusion.

Ray's writing above shows that there is more certainty in images than in words whether that be science, philosophy, or theology. Einstein, in his statement on math and reality, ends exact science: "As far as the laws of mathematics refer to reality, they are not certain, and as far as they are certain, they do not refer to reality". (*The Ultimate Quotable Einstein*, Ed. Alice Calaprice, Princeton University Press, p. 371)

And all of Ray's writings above connects with my central essay "The Declaration of America", in that the certainty of a state combined with the certainty of a religion has not worked. Christianity and Judaism have learned this through their long bloody histories. Islam is next!

I accept the atomistic thinking of the likes of a Epicurus (Greek), Lucretius (Roman), the free thinking of the likes of a Spinoza, and the skepticism of the likes of a Hume.

With Rick Kropf and Ray Macdonald, we have come full circle: A Catholic theologian at the beginning of my investigations and an agnostic and skeptic at my still investigating end. Both are gentlemen and scholars with many questions but few answers (as it should be). Carry on!

A. J. Morse, 6-15-2016

A Recently Rediscovered Book Review

by A. J. Morse

Three groups would benefit greatly from reading Richard Kropf's *The Faith of Jesus: the Jesus of History and the Stages of Faith*. (140 pages; Wipf and Stock Publishers, 2006). The first are adept political followers of current world events, particularly related to religious influence and religious conflict. Through Kropf's history of Jesus, one can understand the difference in the doctrine of the Trinity, which distinguishes Christianity from Judaism and Islam. This difference also brings Kropf to one of his final conclusions: "Religious divisiveness remains one of the greatest, if not the only, cause of human conflict upon this earth. Religion, which should be the greatest unifier of humanity, has become, sadly, almost from the very beginning, a point of contention."

This leads us to the second (and third) group of potential readers: The unbelievers. Using the insights of psychologists like Frankel, Erickson, Fromm, Maslow, Piaget, and Fowler, Kropf shows the development of faith, with all its struggles and doubts, of Jesus who is therefore "a real, suffering and believing human being." Without denying the divinity of Jesus, Kropf accepts the mystery of a wholly human Jesus and believes "that it is much more important to be a Christian — to walk simply and humbly in the footsteps of Jesus, the leader and perfecter of faith." It is not what we believe but how, in faith, we live that is important.

To me, Kropf's book should be of the greatest interest to believers or, more correctly, "true believers." Following up a previous book, *Faith, Security and Risk: the Dynamics of Spiritual Growth* (2003), Kropf says there is always risk taken by the believer and that certainty is a low, undeveloped stage in one's spiritual growth. As a man of much learning and devotional experience, Kropf is always qualifying his deep knowledge in a most Socratic way: "we know very little for sure," "who knows," "we can only speculate," and more. This careful, honest and open approach is not only evidence of Kropf's personal nature, but also shows his awareness of modern biblical "criticism" or scholarship that is, outside a few debunkers, mostly a quest for the real Jesus however it questions historical sources, traditional translations and theological interpretations. This leads him beyond a "hunch" to developmental psychology because "the most obvious historical fact of all is that Jesus of Nazareth was a living person much as the rest of us."

Kropf concludes that "faith, which is a measure of our fundamental trust in God, has been too often and for too long confused with belief or beliefs, which, to a large extent, are views, opinions or attempts to formulate exactly why we may have such trust or confidence."

History confirms that the prophecies and certainties of religious belief with its relative revelations, however divined, can be fancifully fulfilled, however deluded, in destitution and death, however justified. Faith with risks, not belief with certainty, is the trust we must take in God. This is best exemplified by Kropf's Jesus.

(Published in the *Gaylord Herald Times* on September 23, 2006)

47988136R00092

Made in the USA
Lexington, KY
14 August 2019